FUTURES THINKING, LEARNING, AND LEADING

Applying Multiple Intelligences to Success and Innovation

Irving H. Buchen

Rowman & Littlefield Education
Lanham, Maryland • Toronto • Oxford
2006

A ROWMAN & LITTLEFIELD EDUCATION BOOK

Published in the United States of America
by Rowman & Littlefield Education
A Division of Rowman & Littlefield Publishers, Inc.
A wholly owned subsidary of The Rowman & Littlefield Publishing
Group, Inc.
4501 Forbes Boulevard, Suite 200, Lanham, Maryland 20706
www.rowmaneducation.com

PO Box 317
Oxford
OX2 9RU, UK

British Library Cataloguing in Publication Information Available

Library of Congress Cataloging-in-Publication Data

Buchen, Irving H., 1930–
    Futures thinking, learning, and leading : applying multiple intelligences to success
and innovation / Irving H. Buchen.
        p. cm.
    Includes bibliographical references.
    ISBN-13: 978-1-57886-354-9 (hardcover : alk. paper)
    ISBN-13: 978-1-57886-355-6 (pbk. : alk. paper)
    ISBN-10: 1-57886-354-6 (hardcover : alk. paper)
    ISBN-10: 1-57886-355-4 (pbk. : alk. paper)
    1. Diversity in the workplace. 2. Multiple intelligences. 3. Knowledge management.
4. Organizational learning. 5. Creative ability in business. I. Title.
    HF5549.5.M5B825 2006
    658.4'092–dc22   2005029550

∞™ The paper used in this publication meets the minimum requirements of
American National Standard for Information Sciences—Permanence of
Paper for Printed Library Materials, ANSI/NISO Z39.48-1992.
Manufactured in the United States of America.

To Devora

Who gracefully always added caring to the pursuit of the future

CONTENTS

CONTENTS

INTRODUCTION

Education and business may have more in common than either one realizes. For example, both may be facing a tasking and/or diminished future. The pressure for constant academic gains in education and for increases of productivity in business may be approaching the law of diminishing returns. Schools and companies may in fact be encountering the same common outer limits of incremental improvement. In other words, we may be stuck in the successes of past thinking and learning.

The time may thus be ripe to explore a new and expanded definition of educational and corporate intelligence. Multiple intelligences (MI) as part of the larger realm of tapping learning diversity, especially as amplified by recent findings of cognitive science and genetics, may be precisely the quantum jump needed to meet 21st-century global challenges.

THE NEW QUESTIONS AND MEASURES

Typically, intelligence is measured by IQ. The basic question asked is "How smart are you?" The response is numerical. It also displays a hierarchical pecking order. But when successful companies are rated by their smarts and by their intelligence-gathering capacity, the question changes from *how smart they are* to *how they are smart*.

Intelligence is a process, not a static entity. Even in reflection, intelligence is quietly busy. It moves in multiple directions, takes multiple forms, and forms multiple learning linkages. Above all, it can know itself. It can acquire the knowledge of its own operating system so that its dynamics and applications can be optimized or redirected.

Intelligence thus seeks to know how it knows. It does that so that it can not only know how it can know more but also how it can know more differently. It also seeks out the allies of knowing and knowing differently, and how they can extend and even multiply understanding and creativity. Once that incredibly rich world of knowing and how it operates and works is in turn known, it can be self-directed. Thinking, in turn, can manage and amplify its own thinking and learning.

For intelligence to function and flourish, it also needs congenial and challenging external environments. Organizations that craft cultures that welcome and task intelligence not only attract and keep the best and the brightest but also enjoy the competitive edge of next-generation innovation.

But how do professionals and organizations reach such creative goals? One answer is radical basics—to go back to square-one essentials of how we think, learn, and innovate. As noted, the conventional measure of intelligence has been the traditional IQ. But in 1983 in his book *Frames of Mind*, Howard Gardner of Harvard challenged the singularity of linguistic intelligence by claiming there was not one but many intelligences. Moreover, through his research with brain-damaged patients he was able to link and document each intelligence to specific learning pathways of the brain. He identified seven (later eight) intelligences. He referred to MI as the "optimal taxonomy of learning human capacities" and thus provided the human potential movement with a new and more scientific lease on life.

APPLICATIONS

In the past 20 years, education has embraced MI. Books and articles on MI have created an extensive research bibliography, curricula materials and activities have proliferated, and differentiated assessments—especially that of portfolios—have been created to match the diversity of MI. A number of schools at all levels have become dedicated MI schools. And it has worked. Such schools have even handsomely survived the high-stakes testing of No Child Left Behind.

But five major changes and challenges have come about since then:

1. The ante has been upped for both education and business. No longer is minimum performance acceptable. Annual progress in education finds its business match in stretch goals of increasing productivity. Incremental gains are harder to find; even then, such tweaking may fall far short of meeting standards or global competition. Increasingly, the call is not just for improvement but innovation.

2. Since 1983 there has been a significant expansion of brain research and examination of the human genome. The growth of cognitive science and genetic applications clearly raises the question of its impact on thinking and learning in general and on MI in particular. Thus, linking and integrating MI with the findings of cognitive science and genetics is one of the key tasks of this book. What will emerge is an amplification of MI or MI-Plus.

3. There has been virtually no application of MI to business during the same period. That omission may be driven by the fact that it was adopted almost exclusively by education, which limited its application. After all, Gardner is an educational psychologist. Sadly, too, the general disdain business has for education may have led to questioning the value of MI. But the current and future demand for innovation may make business more open to the problem-solving and creative power of MI. And it could not come at a better time when employee testing is reaching for higher state-of-the-art diagnostics for training and performance. Factoring in MI at this juncture may help to introduce the radical basics of the way we think, learn, and innovate and demonstrate the human resources and business applications of MI.

4. A new argument is surfacing: that thinking and learning is also leading, and that thoughtful professionals generally follow the lead of those who think and learn. It is a mutual meritocracy. When all

three processes employ multiple avenues, they enrich and extend each other in many directions and facets. They also become increasingly inclusive and communicative. No one is left out; no intelligence is ignored.

5. Increasingly specialization, while necessary, has led to the loss of the big picture. In addition, the capacity to perceive the integration of parts has often been compromised by rigid structures and work environments. It is a major effort just to see the whole child or employee in all his or her complexity and difference. But the ambitious goal of MI is to simulate 360 degrees—to reflect the total thinking and learning process holistically. At any given time or task, we may not be using all that is there, but to obscure the full potential of what is there is to compromise future wholeness.

To a large extent, the future of changing change is not only compelling but also shaping the recognition and application of learning diversity. The net result is "Futures Thinking, Learning, and Leading" (FTLL), insistently proactive and interoperable. At the heart of the new linkage are minimally three new operating basics:

1. The rejection of singular intelligence for multiple intelligences and learning pathways. All of us are multimodal.
2. The cracking of the genetic code and the formulation of a new interdependent partnership between nature and nurture. All of us are free and determined.
3. The findings of cognitive science and brain research are generating a profile of a richer and fuller potential for development. All of us possess learning diversity.

What this work is therefore about is suggesting the greater range, richness, and diversity of our thinking, learning, and leading, especially as they are amplified and shaped by future demands. Indirectly, this is also a book about leadership, and the new breed of learning leaders who are building a new partnership between intelligence and innovation. In other words, one way of better managing and coping with turbulence is to get a firmer grip on the thinking, learning, and leading tools and methodologies that in fact have contributed to and defined the difference of our fluxy times.

The advantage of focusing on how we think, learn, and lead is that it may provide just the tools we need to better understand and manage changing change. It also introduces the current older generation to what and how their children may be thinking, learning, and leading. Such demographics may in fact offer the most tangible version not only of what is to come but also how the future will conduct and direct its education and business.

I

DEFINING A NEW FUTURE

1

DISTURBING THE FUTURE: MILLENARIAN IGNORANCE AND ARROGANCE

Increasingly, the future is disturbing. It makes us fearful of what is to come. It creates anxiety about continuity and whether we will remain secure and successful, and hold onto our market share. Above all, we are troubled by the prospect of large-scale disasters, bigger and more encompassing, almost planetary in dimension. Two recent examples rapidly come to mind.

First, there was the Y2K problem. Many assurances were given that it would essentially be fixed by 2000. There might be a few lurches here and there but they could be weathered. Meanwhile, there was a sharp increase on the Internet of sales of home safes and emergency supplies of food and drink. Did the future create the problem or did we? Moreover, once the future is disturbed, the responses are predictable. In other words, the loss of management of our own affairs ultimately turned out to be a loss of management of the future. The problem of Y2K thus was compounded. The future became an unwilling partner of our ineptitude. We have somehow stepped over the line.

Another example is the number of recent articles warning of a major recession in the United States: "We have had too much of a good thing too long." "The stock market bears no reality to the economic situation." "Do you really think the world can collapse around us and we remain an absolute island of prosperity?" "How much longer can the wizard of the Fed save us?"

What happens when we begin to worry out loud and in print about a possible future event? Typically, the future is assumed to be a passive agent, a tabula rasa on which projections can be written. But if we go further and in effect set up a self-fulfilling prophecy, the future becomes more agitated, more participatory. The future with its strong sense of history and its limits becomes a stronger, more interventionist player. And the generic fear of uncertainty bestows its intensity on the specific fear of economic collapse.

All this is by way of suggesting that the future is not just an alter ego but also an ego in its own right. It has an identity and a substance other than what we attribute to it. It is this absolute separateness and integrity of the future that needs to be respected and preserved. There is a need to probe the mysteries, principles, laws, and behaviors of the future that we are generally ignorant of—to our potential peril. Otherwise, our ignorance can become arrogance.

AVAILABILITY OF THE FUTURE

Forecasting itself is not always neutral. It fact, it is often another way of disturbing or manipulating the future. This is true especially if the forecasts are egocentric and assume that the forecast is already the future. When there is concern, typically it concerns how good we are as fortune-tellers. How much rigor and substance is there to our methodologies? Seldom, if ever, do we pay attention to our partner's hand. Indeed, our success or failure may rest in part on the extent to which we define the availability of the future to our knowledge.

The future is a mixture of the known, the unknown, and the unknowable. The percentage of each varies with the complexity of the area, the extent of the time line, and the assumptions or presumptions of the forecaster. For example, we know demographically a great deal about the future already, and using straight extrapolation can extend that knowledge far out. We can probably accurately forecast the number of Americans who will reach 100 by the year 3000. Utility companies, in particular in terms of projected energy use, have been involved in these kinds of long-range forecasts for decades, and it has been extremely valuable not only in projecting future use but also in encouraging policies to generate incentives to reduce use. So a significant portion of the future is known. Then, too, that which is unknown is not unknowable. Here is where the forecasters come in. Trend analysis is undertaken, Delphi use of experts generate profiles of future events, probabilities and impacts are assigned as well, and a number of institutional think tanks regularly present their versions of what is to come. These projections along with the demographics make a great deal of the future more available than we have had in the past. But the future is also and absolutely unknowable. Indeed, that is the way the future remains the future. That no-man's-land is the source of the future's potentially retaliatory response. Classically, the presumptuous is an overreacher, a Prometheus, a Faust, a Hitler, and so forth. They all cross over the line to poach on a divine preserve.

So how do we appease the gods? How do we not anger Chronus or Zeus or the science fiction writers? And what kinds of things have we done to date that clearly disturb the universe and that may invite disturbance in return? Basically, they are ecological in nature and planetary in range. We have disturbed the future by pollution, overpopulation, atomic testing, genetic manipulation, and overconsumption. It is not necessary to speculate about the possible bitter fruits our seeds have sown. All the science fictionists, in print and visual forms, have chronicled through their disaster scenarios our future fate. But these warnings are more moralistic than instructive; moreover, they do not help us to define and understand what makes the future tick and be ticked off. They are more egocentric and not sufficiently futuristic; they reflect more anger at human excesses than explain why the future behaves the way it does. In short, they do not have sufficient respect for the laws or principles of future behaviors. So there is a need to increase our knowledge of the way the future responds to what we put upon it.

THE LAW OF CRASH IS SLIP

We already have discussed the way in which the future is a mixture of the known, the unknown, and the unknowable. To that has to be added the awareness of at least two more insights. Both have to do with understanding and even explaining how the future operates and especially how it operates in response to our ignorance. In particular, the future abhors excess. Like a self-indulgent parent, it will put up with a great deal of its offspring's wantonness. Thus, when Meadows and Forrester developed a global computer model to determine what might be the carrying capacity of the planet, the numbers they generated were not as important as the metaphor for a law that binds together both humans and the future. There are limits to growth. They followed by seizing upon the crushing burden of excess population to proclaim: "There is no human goal that requires more people to achieve it." Whatever applications both these powerful admonitions might apply to global leaders and planners, I believe they also were describing immutable laws of the way the future operates. The value of ascribing these behaviors to the future is that they are nonnegotiable.

Another key metaphor of the future appeared over 25 years ago in Garrett Hardin's seminal "Tragedy of the Commons" (1968). Here, too, although the focus was on the unknowing and self-centered action of each person adding just one more sheep to feed at the commons, it also dramatized that the future is an accountant. It monitors excess. The law of crash is slip. Things just don't collapse, they weaken piece by piece. When I was young on a farm, we dumped in the river. But the limit was "You need one mile of clear water between you and your neighbor." The moment you alter those variables—distance, clarity of the water, and number of neighbors—the river may become a liquid commons. Clearly, the future is not unlimited. Its capacity to accommodate growth, diversity, bounty, and so on is ruled by hidden constraints.

ACCELERATED AND DIMINISHING RETURNS

Another set of laws or behaviors about the future has to do not so much with space but time. How fast is the future? Is it faster than we are? Is it ahead of its schedule? We are so accustomed to describing the most recent decade in terms of rapid change that we are almost numb to its meaning; and presumptuously we even think we control the rate. But an argument can be made that the future has its own clock; indeed, sometimes that mechanism operates at geometric rather than arithmetic rates. When Ray Kurzweil published "Age of Intelligent Machines" in 1990, he invoked the law of accelerating returns. By that, he meant that without being fully aware, humans have struck a Faustian bargain; we have allied and even merged with the technology we created, and we have made the future happen faster and faster. In other words, in Kurzweil's vision, the future embodies our image as a symbiotic machine. What we call the rapid rate of change is really the future incarnating in a rapidly moving present the various incarnations of that image. In other words, the future is not some obedient tabula rasa waiting for humans to make their marks on it but an already active partner in shaping the present. Thus, Kurzweil asks, "When will we consider machine intelligence to be conscious?" He answers, "When the machines tell us." Kurzweil does not react in horror at the possible shift of control. Rather, his assumption is that we have always been in a partnership with the future, both constructive and destructive, only now it is increasingly visible and actualized. So whatever speed we set things in motion, the future will always generate accelerated returns. But that has to be linked to another law of speed—reaction time or the law of diminishing returns.

The future is not inconsiderate or uncaring. In a sense, it is a better communicator of forecasts than we are. It sends messages, warnings, handwritings on the wall, coming attractions—in short, extensive and varied forms of future feedback. But because we do not sufficiently understand that the future's monitoring is also an admonishing function, we do not read or heed the signs. In fact, the future is persistent and provides more than one opportunity for foreknowledge. Specifically, it offers three incremental stages: stretch, strain, and shock. The earliest warning provides the opportunity to take almost routine manageable corrective action. After all, stretch is relatively easy; we all should be able to do that. But if we neglect that opportunity and discount the warning, then the future's law of escalation comes into play. The next stage is strain, more difficult than stretch but still within realm of the possible. But if we ignore that stage, then the future delivers shock. That is grim. Crisis management becomes a norm. The choices available are few, and many are between lesser evils. Think of all the warnings CEOs received over the years before downsizing and did nothing. In short, the future is a "compounder." The law of accelerated returns is coupled with the law of diminishing returns. Both laws are subject to the higher law of escalation.

One final variation on who is in charge. David Post, recently interviewed in *Wired* (Lappin 1998), pushes Kurzweil's notion of the partnership between humans and the future even further. Post claims that humans and the future have taken over from nature the direction of evolution. Indeed, most natural evolution is already over. Besides, genetic manipulation has made nature no longer a master but a handmaiden of human design: "Evolution is a search algorithm to find higher and higher positions on a fitness landscape" (Lappin 1998). To Post, humans left to their own designs cannot ever bring to the task of evolutionary direction the scale and grandeur of vision that the future has. Post thus argues that the future can deliver "aggregate happiness" and "species differentiation." In short, there is no competition. Besides, the future alone can save or protect humans from their baseness, littleness, and lack of imagination, and the arrogance of anthropomorphic ignorance. No wonder Kurzweil and Post are so eager to support an incremental partnership with the future and to argue for a deeper understanding of its role.

NEW SYSTEMS, NEW METAPHORS, NEW STRUCTURES

Knowing the future is not like "knowing thy enemy," because the future is not the enemy unless provoked. And as noted so far, that occurs mostly because of ignorance of the future's ways. But the most significant yield of this acquired knowledge is that it invites reformulation. We already have noted how Meadows and Forrester's notion of the limits to growth and that of the tragedy of the commons can bring about a new way of conceiving and working with the future. The same holds true for the notions of speed and the promise of partnership. But to these should be added the development of new systems to manage human and economic affairs that are different and more in sympathy with the nature of the future's systems. Two significant new metaphors come to mind, one urged by Margaret Wheatley, the other by Tachi Kiuchi.

Both follow a traditional route up to a point. Both look for a system of organization in nature that might better apply to human organizations than the standard hierarchies developed by Taylor (1911) and others and symbolized by pyramidal organizational charts. Their unhappiness with current structures is that they are too controlling or too leery of any degree of management supervision and intervention that cannot manage change, complexity, and rapid speed. Without saying it in so many words, they want an organizational structure that is not fixed, centrist, or hierarchical because they believe that is not what the future demands because that is not what the structure of the future is. Both want systems that are self-organizing, self-designing, and self-creating with little or no time lag between stimulus and response.

For Wheatley and Kellner-Rogers (1996), it is the metaphor of the river that moves at different speeds and has no final or lasting shape but in mercurial fashion alters as the terrain does. It is thus self-propelled, and whatever shape it has at any given moment is a temporary fusion of the impulse of the river and the demands of the external environment. The end goal remains fixed: to empty into the sea. That is the desired fulfillment of all rivers. For Wheatley, the law of the future is the survival of the most flexible; anything fixed in stone is an anathema to Wheatley and the future. Monuments and monumental organizations will be the version of the dinosaurs—future pyramids. Recently, Charles Handy (2002) wove a variation on Wheatley's notion by describing an organizational core of about 100 professionals who constituted a mobile, agile, and multidisciplinary steering group. Handy's goal was to give centralized direction to a decentralized, self-organizing corps.

For Kiuchi, it is the rain forest because of its capacity for embracing almost endless diversity and because its capital lies in its design. The incredible variety and creativity of the rain forest according to Kiuchi (1997) is that it is a brain forest—an enormously complicated series of interconnections of species and synapses that are constantly in synch and out of synch with each other, every second, without end. To Kiuchi the great lesson of the rain forest and the law of the future is interconnectivity, nature's cyber network. As CEO of Mitsubishi Electric, Kiuchi promptly began implementing the laws of the future by physically putting together divisions and units that had been separated, and by requiring units that seldom had any contacts with each other to establish regular and closer relations. The only element missing from Kiuchi's new configuration is the self-organizing principle of Wheatley's river—but for that to happen Kiuchi himself would have to be less the CEO and more the anonymous navigator of the river.

In summary, then, what are the essential characteristics and laws of the future?

1. The future is more available and less available to forecasting and knowledge than we customarily think. It is a mixture of the known, the unknown (but not unknowable), and the unknowable (which is absolutely unknowable). The future is disturbed only when its final limits are not respected. Then retaliation is swift.
2. The future abhors excess of any kind. It embodies limits of various kinds—above all, limits to growth. In a sense it keeps a perpetual running tab of all that is going on. It counts the number of sheep added to the commons. Many look around in bewilderment and wonder why the commons ended. The answer is gradually.
3. The future is always in high gear. It is not just fast but offers constantly accelerated returns. As an antidote, however, it also offers anticipatory warnings—stretch, strain, and shock—which provide sufficient response time unless they are ignored; in that case, accelerated returns are compounded by diminishing returns. But the law of escalation is as formidable as it is inevitable.
4. Although both humans and nature are now engaged in evolution, the genetic designer is the future. All the new configurations will take place under auspices of the future as science fiction becomes a norm.
5. Finally, the future is receptive, knowledgeable, and communicative about the new designs for organizations that seek optimum self-organizing interconnectivity. Such organizations externally and internally will be both more competitive and cooperative. Their shapes will also be evolving and changing, producing fluid organizations that in effect have a river running through them. Above all, our knowledge about the laws of the future will make us eligible to be its equal partner. And that, in fact, will be our distinction in the years to come.

REFERENCES

Handy, Charles. 2002. *The elephant and the flea: Reflections of a reluctant capitalist*. Boston, Mass.: Harvard Business School Press.

Hardin, Garrett. 1968. The tragedy of the commons. *Science* 162: 1,243–48.

———. 1998. Extensions of "The tragedy of the commons." *Science* 280 (May 1): 682–83.

Kiuchi, Tachi. 1997. *Lessons from the rain forest*. Paper presented at the annual meeting of the World Future Society, San Francisco.

Kurzweil, Ray. 1990. *Age of intelligent machines*. Cambridge, Mass.: MIT Press.

Lappin, Todd. 1998. Interview with David Post: The missing link. *Wired* 6 (August).

Malone, Thomas, Michael Morton, and Rossman Halperin. 1996. Organizing for the 21st century. *Strategy and Leadership* (Strategic Leadership Forum) 24 (July–August): 7–10.

Meadows, Donella H. et al. (paperback reissue) 1974. *The limits to growth: A report for the Club of Rome's Project on the Predicament of Mankind*. Basingstoke, U.K.: Pan Macmillan.

Taylor, Frederick W. 1911. *The principles of scientific management*. New York: Harper & Bros.

Wheatley, Margaret, and Myron Kellner-Rogers. 1996. Self-organization, strategy and leadership. *Strategy and Leadership* (Strategic Leadership Forum) 24 (July–August): 18–24.

2

FUTURE AGENDAS:
THE SCIENCE FICTION MODEL

Traditionally, organizations pursue the future. Now the future seems to be pursuing companies—in some cases, into the ground. E-businesses appear and disappear with almost daily regularity, or they are acquired, subsumed, and are no longer. Even big and traditional organizations no longer have a singular or familiar shape. They spawn incubators, new divisions, offshore offshoots or outsourced variations, and so on. Structurally they resemble planets of different sizes and speeds in a solar system more than they do the traditional pyramidal wedding cake monolith. Young MBA whiz kids major in entrepreneurship.

Why does the future appear to be arriving ahead of schedule? Are we provoking it into happening prematurely by being Promethean, or worse, like Daedalus flying too close to the sun? In other words, is there the presumption, as some moralists would argue, that it is being brought about by overreaching? Or are the shorter time periods between discovery and implementation simply the result of a neutral phenomenon? Whatever the answer, the real issue is neither blame nor innocence but an understanding of the characteristics of a fast future so that we may better manage it.

Historically, the future was better behaved. It waited for us to come to it. It did not have a mind or agenda of its own. It was there obediently ready to serve and to be around as an affirmation of our continuance. Often it had great political or economic value. What could not happen totally or immediately could be put off or gradualized. Of course, it also served to afflict both the faithful and the godless. After all, the second coming was always seeking a future date of incarnation. In short, as long as the future stayed in its place, it could serve a multitude of purposes and overlays. It was ultimately a servant, there to do our bidding.

THE FUSION OF SCIENCE FICTION AND THE FUTURE

But we also know that there were historical quantum jumps that opened the cage of the future and released a beast ready to pounce. Again and again stealing the fire of invention mythically and metaphorically marked one of those shifts. Eating of the tree of knowledge marked another. The printing press in preserving and releasing the past from oblivion also liberated the future. Technology in general increasingly became the midwife of major discontinuities. Science fiction appeared with Mary Shelley's *Frankenstein*. It celebrated the first of many fusions of mind and machine, intelligence and artifice.

Since that time, there has been a steady and parallel race between science fiction and the future. Sometimes the one leading, sometimes the other, but the two have been permanently in contention or acting in collusion. Indeed, science fiction embodies such a total pursuit of the future of us that it is difficult to determine where the one begins and the other leaves off. But in any case, science fiction may provide a key model for managing fast futures. Constantly exhorted to fight fire with fire, perhaps the way to engage and manage a fast future is to employ a fast future form.

Science function (SF) minimally provides three managerial guidelines: stance, scenario, and solution.

Stance

The most basic stance of SF is that the future has already arrived. It is not only the key setting but also the main protagonist. SF stands unequivocally in its midst. The future is thus not just coyly visited but intensely portrayed. Readers experience a future world in the present time and place of fiction. In addition, much of the drama may stem from the future dynamically envisioning its own future. Whether it is glorious or disastrous, it firmly establishes that the future has a future.

Managers and strategic planners like SF have to be time travelers. They cannot timidly and obediently stand in the present and peer out at what is to come. They must abandon their secure moorings and assumptions and allow themselves to drift into a time and place that never existed before. The only way strategic planners can withstand and understand the pursuit by the future is to inhabit and engage where the future is coming from in the first place. Although the future may still be a moving target, it now nevertheless is a tangible entity that can be examined.

Scenario

If God is in the details, in Zen, understanding is to be found in observing the way a wise man ties his shoes. SF is a second creation story. In SF, although it can be largely fantastic and even wild, scenario also makes the outlandish appear familiar. As Marianne Moore noted, poetry is an imaginary garden in which there is a real toad. Similarly, SF has to present a reality that offers verisimilitude, the substance and stuff of recognizable existence, and the external and internal consistency and coherency of real people and situations. In short, imagination always needs, like Antaeus, to have its feet on the ground, otherwise it loses its power and impact.

Managers mistakenly use tunnel vision to look and plan ahead. They are so preoccupied with their own special focus that the future appears monochromatic and familiar. By limiting their views to only what they believe will affect their organization, their vision invariably appears myopic, singular, and safe.

They must also examine alternative events and dimensions, like the proverbial rock thrown into a pool sending out wider and wider ripples. In the process they may discover wider, deeper, and unexpected applications, way beyond what their more compulsively singular competitors have found. In short, inhabiting the future is not enough. It must also be a rich unexpected world, one that is dizzily strange yet logical.

Solution

Science function is fundamentally a problem-posing and problem-solving genre. To be sure, sometimes the solutions are terminal; given the problem, that may be a logical conclusion. If well-crafted, the solution appears inevitable. In good SF, many solutions are proposed and debated. Discussions, sometimes heated, take place; their purpose is to eliminate options until one absolutely final solution appears as the remaining and winning contender. Whether the ending is an unhappy or wrenching one, there is at least the consolation of all possibilities being exhausted. The work that comes to such a well-rounded end has about it the ring of inevitable truth.

SF AND MANAGERIAL SOLUTIONS

The best of SF thus sets high standards for managerial solutions.

Nothing cheap, trivial, or lame will pass muster. In this case, life needs to imitate art. Following the problem-solving methodology of SF, minimally every solution has to be perceived as passing five standards. First, the solution must solve the problem—the whole problem, and nothing but the problem. Second, the problem cannot be reworked or reduced in magnitude because the solution is not big enough to handle it all. Third, the solution must not become a later problem. Fourth, it must be communicable—persuasive and lifelike to secure acceptance and cooperation. Finally, it must take hold and be implementable, not in some future time and place, but now in the present culture; and if not, what would it take to make it fit snugly and securely?

The SF process is exhaustively circular. The end point of future speculation must always bend back to connect to the beginning points of the present. Ultimately, they may appear one and the same with genesis becoming terminus and terminus, genesis. The SF problem trajectory requires managers to take the high road of generating solutions that are robust, rigorous, and renewable. Above all, the fast future of SF compels managers to recognize that they are dealing with a rapid reality that has a mind and timetable of its own.

If one views the difference of the future as an adversary to be beaten or a competitor to be bested, that will not yield the value of transforming an enemy into an ally. A begrudging captive will not reveal as much as a liberated colleague. In short, confronting a fast future is a challenge of discontinuous growth unlike any other.

SF offers managers a model of living in the future, creating or recreating its world and laws in all their fantastic tangibility, mastering the tasking standards and circular process of higher-level problem posing and problem solving, and testing applicability with its final embodiments of communication and implementation. Finally, all managers should reread Mary Shelley's *Frankenstein* and discover that the creature snatched from the future had no name.

3

SHAPING FUTURE AGENDAS: THE FUTURISTS' MODEL

As a profession, futurists have sharpened and extended the tools and techniques of strategic planning and forecasting. They also have often spelled out the writing on the wall and frequently have provided early warning and opportunity data and trends. They may lament that they are not used or recognized as much as they would like, but they know the risks that attend looking ahead and the discomforts it may engender. Earl Joseph summed that sentiment up recently when he responded to the question of how he could tell how well a futures presentation he made was received: "They don't invite you back."

It is understandable. If we are good at what we do, we are often not reassuring. Forecasts obviously may extrapolate and build on historical and evolutionary patterns and trends, but if they only do that and fail to address the discontinuous they are not genuinely futuristic. Thinking about the future thus employs a different kind of thinking and questioning, at odds with the status quo. It does not accept the latest development as the final position. It involves always taking the next step, traveling down the road not taken, extending the trajectory to its as yet unnamed landing place.

If the answer is not transformational, then futurists are superfluous. We are not timeservers. We name and preside over gulfs and gaps. We

are normally and routinely radical. Created by the turbulence of discon-
nection, futurists nevertheless anticipate and point to the emergence of
new bridging norms whose clarity may somewhat redeem future shock.

But futurists may now have to pause and reaffirm their mission in the
21st century. The failure of many leaders has brought about a resurgence
of a timid present. We are preoccupied with defining the blind spots of
CEOs when the basic one is that they were all myopically present-bound.
They may have given lip service to the predictable partnerships between
productivity and technology, but they were blind to the trinity of global-
ity, futurity, and creativity, let alone their interoperability.

It is time to take stock and redefine our focus if we are to preserve our
identity and define our value and contribution. Above all, the minimum
methodological range of futurist inquiry and discourse needs to be described and prescribed. There is a need to step back and establish the
essential directional requirements of processing future issues and extent. In short, we need to review and restate our taxonomy as a profession and discipline if we are truly to reflect our difference to ourselves
and to others.

But why especially now? What are the driving urgencies? We have
come to the end of incrementalism. Distress is not symptomatic but systemic. The complexity of interconnectedness is bewildering. In other
words, the current conditions of the future are demanding a correspon-
ding response. The three dimensions proposed below suggest the minimum portals for processing and futurizing current issues. Others obviously can be proposed, but these may be sufficient to stir debate about
the criteria futurists must apply to justify the acceptance of issues on a
futures agenda.

1. *Global Framing*. The framework must be both national and global.
   The traffic between the two has to be extensively monitored, but
   it cannot be solely or primarily nationalistically driven. Such ego-
   centricity needs to be resisted and replaced by reciprocity. For example, how will the Chinese love affair with the American MBA
   express itself in the culture of Chinese business? How will those
   applications compare and contrast with American versions? And
   how are both patterns part of a larger context? The rise and fall of
   empires and cultures is, after all, not a singular but a cyclical

process. Framing has to always exceed and be bigger than its parameters.

2. *Converging*. This is the wild card. This is where the total may be
greater than the sum of its parts. This is where the singular reigns,
where Edward Wilson's (1998) "consilience" appears like an extraterrestrial visitor from outer space. It not only links the soft and
the hard (sociology and biology) but also the psychological and
physiological (brain research and the genetic code). Nature versus
nurture has become nature via nurture. Although no one would
claim that futurists enjoy special insights here, they do or should
enjoy two edges. First, by virtue of being both generalists and specialists, they are better positioned to discern convergence in the
big and the small. Second, they need to insist that the issue of convergence be addressed as part of the process of elevating any item
to a futures agenda.

3. *New Breed of the Generalist Specialist*. It is not enough to talk to
and write only for specialists. The global has to be rendered lo-
cally; the conceptual has to be communicated in narrative terms.
This means that the communication of the big and interconnected picture has to not only be written but portrayed, displayed, and visualized. All futurists have to become science fiction writers or minimally learn and master the art of scenarios
and simulations.

Whatever their individual specialization, futurists have to acquire the
generic ability to translate numbers and patterns into real time, real situations, and real people. Nor should this be perceived as an automatic
add-on without contributory value. Communication gives forecasts the
third degree. It essentially tasks and tests the contemplated projection
as to its communicability. In many ways, that really measures its viabil-
ity and validity. And if it fails then perhaps it needs to be returned to the
drawing board and revised.

In other words, communication is not mere word-smithing but needs
to become an integral futurist tool. It is the litmus test of forecasting fidelity. But it has another value. It habituates audiences and recipients of
coming attractions to insist that the fine print be spelled out. It helps
thus to build a more demanding audience of and for the future.

Is a futures agenda of the future a monopoly of futurists? Obviously not, but it would be wise to employ at least one or two to review and critique it. They may save your future. Futurists are experts at sins of omission, premature time lines, limited complexity, and above anticipatory timidity. They have the vision to preserve not only your lunch and dinner but also perhaps your food chain. They also can model what a generic futures agenda should look like and contain.

The characteristics of a futurist agenda include:

1. A genuine futures agenda is always interventionist.
2. Forecasts themselves are interventionist events.
3. Collaborating with what is projected is required.
4. Constant and overlapping partnerships between the now and the then have to be forged.
5. The agenda must combine data and story and straddle the present artifacts of this world with the scenarios of what is yet to be.

Finally, the above also offers a special kind of futures insurance. Futurists would never allow future subjects to be listed, as they often are, as the last items of the agenda where they regularly suffer the fate of running out of time and being undiscussed. When that happens—when it is followed by the customary timeserving comment, "Let's carry over those items to the next meeting; they will keep until then"—then it is time to bring in a futurist and his or her model agenda.

A futurist will help forge a genuine forward-looking agenda in which the future not only is the first but also may be the only item on the agenda. A futurist would never allow the future to be dispossessed of its cutting and disturbing edge or its position of absolute priority. In short, in a futurist agenda, the future always calls the shots. It is in charge. It is the CEOF.

REFERENCE

Wilson, Edward. 1998. *Consilience: The unity of knowledge*. New York: Knopf.

4

"THE GREAT CONVERGENCE": VISIONARY ILLUSION OR MEGATREND?

It is usual to treat Leonardo as a scientist and as a painter in separate studies. And no doubt the difficulties in following his mechanical and scientific investigations make this a prudent course. Nevertheless, it is not completely satisfactory, because in the end the history of art cannot be properly understood without some reference to the history of science. In both we are studying the symbols by which man affirms his mental scheme, and these symbols, be they pictorial or mathematical, a fable or a formula, will reflect the same changes.

—Kenneth Clark, *Leonardo da Vinci* (1990)

Every major forecasting effort of the past 25 years always has exhibited an intellectual core—a global concept of transformation. To the traditional history of ideas, forecasters have added the history of future ideas. Indeed, it is the task of futurists, acknowledged or not, to preside at historical branch points and to identify the future implications, directions, and choices provided by and compelled by the emergence of powerful megatrends. The key task has always been to discover the major forces in the present that are driving future development. Is what appears to be emerging now a resurgence of the pursuit of unified knowledge? What is there about the current situation and the next two decades that is pressuring and presaging a preoccupation with the integration and unification of all knowledge? Who are some of the major figures and what are the shaping factors that individually and collectively help to determine whether the content generated has the conceptual power to function as a megatrend?

Three representative areas of convergent thought will be examined. The first deals with the technology and theology of convergence, the second with the socioeconomic and political dimensions of "connexity," and the third with the "consilience" of science and the humanities. Finally, a summary of the range and substance of those three areas should serve to establish the basis for designating convergence as a megatrend of the third millennium.

CONVERGENCE: TECHNOLOGY AND THEOLOGY

According to Gary Schwartz, "the universe of one science" presupposes a constellation of common research inquiries and activities. There is always the many before there is the one. Gradually, however, discrete and scattered strands of inquiry coalesce, become initially a cluster and then a consortium of cross-fertilization, and finally converge and emerge as a powerful force with a common theoretical and intellectual agenda. To make sense of this dynamic progression and to provide reassuring tangibility, the future is often rendered as a new creation story or science fiction focused on the specifics of creating, for example, autonomous humans, amplified and potentially ageless. And so begins the sometimes uneasy partnership between technology and theology.

Peter Cochrane (1999) describes two frontiers that already have been crossed. The first involves what he calls the "internal pharmacy" by which humans can be maintained at an individualized optimum level automatically. A metabolic profile is developed for each individual, and to it are pegged all known medications as well as chemicals and nutrient supplements to maintain optimum balance. When implanted, it monitors the various functions and vital signs that are to be maintained and dispenses the appropriate chemical in the appropriate amount to maintain efficacy.

All of this builds on new implant and sustained release technology of drugs or electrical charges that are disease-specific (cancer or diabetes).

As a result there is already considerable expertise and even familiarity with the procedures. But what Cochrane claims is a quantum jump is that it is based on a total understanding of the interacting and integrating dynamics of the entire human system. It is that convergence of knowledge that provides the intellectual base for producing a complete metabolic profile of each individual. Perhaps, its greatest value (given genetic predictors and family history) is to provide proactive options to be involved in preventive medicine.

The second convergence of this magnitude is what Cochrane calls the creation of "the third intelligence." In his *Tips for Time Travelers* (1994), he discusses information overload, certainly not new. Cochrane seeks not a temporary fix but a permanent solution. Incremental knowledge only adds to the overload. What is needed is pattern recognition of knowledge patterns and paths between and across knowledge areas. Only such models of integrated knowledge clusters can then comprehend multiple reverberating effects of drug interactions, the dynamics of global pollution and recovery, and finally, thinking in 10 dimensions. But easier said than done: how do we get there?

Cochrane outlines the research agenda. Our technology needs to undergo a double development. First, it has to be given a range of sensory inputs (with enough blank space to accommodate more); second, the neural ability to create its own perceptions. Development along cloning lines is not the way to go. That is the incremental direction. What Cohrane seeks is an interfacing chip that can understand the way we think and conceive and yet possesses its own intelligence, which is intentionally different and even divergent. It is a permeable relationship, sometimes equal, sometimes not; sometimes one dominating, sometimes the other, and sometimes neither. But although the fit—initially, at least—has to be mutual and consensual, it must be allowed to develop on the one hand and to call on other means when the problem exceeds the combined power and comprehension of the third intelligence on the other hand. In short, the projected convergence requires human-technological intervention in the evolution of the species—a new Adam and Eve—with the midwife being unlimited synthesis.

But is it doable? Federico Faggin (1997), who was instrumental in developing the first microprocessor and cofounder of Synaptics, agrees with Ray Kurzweil (1993): "In the human brain there is no distinction between hardware and software. The biological neural networks of the brain are instead special kind of intelligent hardware that is not completely fixed at birth but evolves and modifies with time as the person grows and learns." In other words, part of the daunting complexity of the brain is that it is already integrated—already hardware and software—whereas our current intelligent machines are dualistic. Then, too, not only do the neural networks of the brain change with patterns of use and experience but also in the process generate "the mind," which is a combined creation of the brain with information and learning. Increasingly the brain and the mind develop a master–servant relationship. In other words, it is no small matter to design "brain chips," but it is an incredibly difficult task to design "mind chips." Finally, the brain-mind is a "self-programming, self-learning, and self-managing system. It is autonomous." Interestingly, Faggin calls the material of this new technological development "clay": "Reconfigurable hardware, once programmed for sufficient autonomy, has about it the promise of being self-regulating, thus supportive of precisely the way the mind thinks and learning proceeds. The test of whether it is a successful mimic of the mind is whether it helps to develop information impact." And, according to Claude Shannon (cited in Burke 1997), the father of information theory, "Information causes change. If it doesn't it is not information."

Sometimes, the applications and objects of projected convergences surface even before the theoretical and intellectual convergence knowledge base has fully solidified. James Burke has compiled a significant number of examples. One occurred after the Civil War and involved the convergence of piano and firearms technology to produce the first rudimentary typewriter. Although Burke gives a number of other examples, he maintains that to be authentically convergent a new law of math must be operative—one plus one equals three: "The results of convergence is greater than the sum of its parts" (1999, 97). In fact, Burke argues that the absence of surprise indicates that convergence is not operative.

Burke finally is so persuaded that the forces of synthesis will bring about incredible change that he explicitly crosses over from technology to theology by calling it the "Great Convergence." It will be finally an assault on creationism and divine beginnings. In the process, science increasingly will sound like religion, but that is not totally surprising. In fact, if nature were not so profound to begin with, science would not exist at all. There would be nothing to explain, no patterns to be found, no order to be discovered. The classic comment by Einstein is correct: "The most incomprehensible thing about the universe is that it is comprehensible." Thus, according to Burke, science's quest for convergence is really and always a quest for the origins of all things. In this connection, the human genome is the mother lode. It offers re-creation. It should be recalled in this connection that Faggin spoke about the new multigated chips as clay in the hands of the potter. For Burke, then, much of the intellectual novelty and power of the great convergence is that it will finally bring about a fusion of science and religion, Prometheus and God.

Separately, Paul Davies (1994) notes that the scope of current and future scientific inquiry was originally the exclusive preserve of priests and mystics. He also notes that although the issues of the nature and the origins of the laws of nature come from are "strictly speaking, not scientific but metaphysical questions," that separation is no longer respected or valued. Although Davies does not oppose the coming of the great convergence or warn of dire consequences if it succeeds, not so the misgivings of Mark Helprin.

Helprin (1999) raises three major objections. First, what have been called *patterns of coming together* occur all the time in nature and just as often come asunder. But to invest the occasional or even frequent patterns of convergence with the force of a total and permanent arrangement is to inflate the significance of partial occurrence with a reassurance that just is not there. Not unlike Stephen Jay Gould who in his *Full House* (1996) argues that man is not unique, Helprin maintains that evolution operates not by progress but by diversity and variation and there are many species of Homo sapiens. Helprin also argues that the complexity of human design and human society is greater than that of nature. The number of variables is so great that it cannot be understood, let alone managed. Finally, the great convergence really seeks to attack the last great frontier and to take on time itself. It is nothing less than the ultimate presumption of immortality.

Does Helprin have a case? Of course he does, but the first two objections are really challenges, not absolute denials. He may turn out to be correct in both assumptions, in which case the great convergence will either have to make some adjustments or not be that great or converging.

The last issue is a real one, but the proponents of convergence are not willing at this point to contemplate anything so absolute or arrogant. In effect they are really talking about longevity or relative immortality not an absolute condition. But what is dramatically clear is that the new technology born of convergence is in effect a theology. Indeed, the ultimate synthesis may be to make them one.

CONNEXITY

Helprin's misgivings about understanding and managing human and societal complexity is in fact a central focus of Geoff Mulgan, who directs a think tank, teaches at University College in London, and is, most important for our focus, a member of Prime Minister Tony Blair's Policy Unit. The title of his book, *Connexity* (1997), not only introduces a new and futuristic term to the discussion of synthesis but also takes a new direction. Mulgan's concern is with culture, especially the culture of politics, government, and social change. His contribution to and reinforcement of the theory of convergence is thus offered from a social science perspective.

To Mulgan, human history basically has been preoccupied by three major definitions of the sociopolitical self. All three currently coexist in different countries, societies, and classes because the world is a total time machine. The first one is the culture of dependence in which freedom is in very short supply and a single dominant and dominating ideology and theology is tyrannically in place. Deservedly, maintains Mulgan, wherever that kind of bondage prevails it is appropriately designated as the dark ages. Happily, declarations of independence, through both revolution and evolution, ushered in a culture not only of democratic, egalitarian, and proactive discourse but also of unbridled and unshackled inquiry. Indeed, it is from this emancipation that the twins of democracy and science emerged and flourished. But Mulgan finds substantial evidence for the emergence of a third or new phase: interdependence. Like the phases that preceded it, interdependence came about as an antidote to excessive freedom and to the notion of the self as sovereign.

In conditions and cultures of freedom, the individual rules supreme and feels free to call upon all the means of his society to protect and even increase his freedom, especially when anything appears to challenge, contain, or abridge it. The net result is an ambiguously liberating and self-indulgent society of freewheeling, self-contained, autonomous individuals whose orbits are unrestrained and undirected. That is basically a win/lose process in which the self wins but social coherence loses. But what Mulgan sees increasingly emerging are individuals and societies that increasingly accept that they are connected to everyone and everything else and they exist in a "web of mutual interdependence . . . they are evolving towards a higher integration" (1997, 17). The alternative culture increasingly accepted and encouraged by both psychologists and sociologists is one in which "the self is perceived less as given, less complete, less whole. . . . Maturing means accepting your incompleteness, your permeability to other people" (52).

Although Mulgan clearly favors this new image of the self in an increasingly interconnected society, he sees it as largely voluntary in Western cultures and more of a tradition in Eastern cultures. But he does argue rightly that it is being hastened on the one hand by need and by enlightenment on the other. Thus, the incredible commitment in business to interdependent teams is being driven by intense competition and by the capacity of teams to be more innovative. Indeed, that "teamness" is celebrated by a new term—coopetition—a fusion of cooperation and competition. Compelled or chosen, "habits of association foster virtuous circles of self-organization" (1997, 30–31). In politics and in social reform, it is increasingly recognized that freedom "only works in partnership with other ideals, not on its own" (53). The limits of freedom are more than offset by the benefits of collaboration. The new ideal of the future is a reconstitution of identity, which will take the form of the collectivized individual who encloses self and other in the same person.

Mulgan further identifies three major laws of interconnectedness. The first is generally a corrective. The notion of technological advancement as discrediting what it ostensibly displaces is not borne out by patterns of evidence: "Throughout the twentieth century physical mobility and communications grew in tandem rather than as substitutes" (1997, 28). Electronic culture did not replace books; book sales have increased. In fact, both media appear online in amazon.com. The growth of videoconferencing ironically boosted the market for hotel conference centers. Economists claimed that the 80 percent of economic growth of the

1950s was accounted for by technological change, but studies by Paul Romer (2001) of Stanford University have shown the primary role played by ideas and knowledge growth in driving economic growth.

Thus, "Connexity tends to be cumulative. Each new medium of communication does not replace its predecessors so much as complement them" (Mulgan 1997, 28); connexity rests on the recognition of recurrent coexistence. That is how so-called opposites or disconnects are perceived as being in tandem—as cooperating. Even in science, which tends to regularly throw out the past and to be noncumulative, what is really discarded are the conclusions not the theories; the Greeks still haunts us, as does Darwin.

The second key law of increasing connectedness is the convergence of the world economy and world ecology. The environment has become the supreme advocate of interdependence and compelled a recognition of a single world, without borders and perceived as a single whole from outer space. The same recognition is attributed to the global economy, which is a composite of world trade, world direct investments, global diffusion of technologies, and an integrated communications system. Indeed, the "infosphere" has the same integrated qualities of the biosphere. In fact, Mulgan claims that we need new maps of the world to replace the standard ones of land masses as chosen by political masters:

> Today the links matter as much as the territory, and our maps should show the volume of trade, of messages, or of movements if people. We need maps that can measure the ease of communication or travels in terms of how long it takes to send a message or to move a thing between two points—giving us a map of the world made up of isomorphic lines, rapidly coming closer together over time, until most parts of the world are within twenty-four hours of each other in physical movement, and a few microseconds in terms of the movement of information. (1997, 23)

The intense economics of exchange in a global economy has created world prices for goods and services, where in the past there were only local prices. In fact, that is precisely the source of intimate competition: a plant in Ohio is aware of the price and the quality of the same product made in Korea; and more seriously, so are its customers. *Homo sapiens* is increasingly becoming also *Homo economicus*, a person who defines himself as a series of multiple exchanges, who functions in an interconnected world made up a of a lattice of contracts and reciprocal flows of goods and services. The effort conceptually to master such complexity brought about the reinvention of political economy, which ironically existed as a single discipline in the 19th century and then was split wrongly into political science and economics. As a result, we have political scientists who know nothing about economics and economists who know little about politics. But unified again, the two disciplines have produced a significant body of research that affirms interconnectedness. As Mulgan claims, "Institutions of free trade have proven more effective than those designed to prevent or contain war, and more diplomatic activity is now devoted to managing trade than to managing security" (1997, 59). Global economy is thus as good—if not a better—advocate of peace than the United Nations, which is still a creation of barriers of sovereignty rather than dedicated to their removal by interconnectedness. Another agent of global convergence is ecology. Pressure for ecological integration has become a critical force that acknowledges and defines both.

Finally, Mulgan's third law of convergence or connxeity provides those like himself who are preoccupied with social, political, and economic design with a model to imagine and to design a self-organizing society, as opposed to one made up of separate self-organizing groups, the favorite isolated states of politicos. To Mulgan, the

> philosophical idea that best expresses this ideal of a self-organizing society is autopoiesis, or self-creation, one of the most potent themes in contemporary systems thinking. The Chilean scientists Humberto Maturana and Francisco Varela gave autopoiesis a modern form. They argued that rather than thinking of systems in relation to an external environment we should see them as autonomous, circular, self-referential, primarily concerned with their own organization and identity. (1997, 157)

The creation of a culture of autonomy suggests

> how a society might organize itself, adapting and evolving, without the need for hierarchies and belief systems that stand above people, enforcing continuity and responsibility. If each human life makes the transition from dependence through independence to interdependence,

then . . . societies should make the same transition, evolving into a
common framework within which each element can take responsibility
for itself and for the whole. (158)

To Mulgan, the promise of connexity is thus ultimately utopian.

CONSILIENCE

Perhaps, the supreme spokesperson and articulator of the unification of
all knowledge is Edward O. Wilson. In fact, his last book *Consilience*
(1999) is subtitled "The Unity of Knowledge." In this role, he follows the
lead of Gerald Holton, historian and physicist, who called the pursuit of
the unity of all sciences the "Ionian Enchantment," the roots of which
go back at least to the 6th century B.C. and to Thales of Miletus, who,
according to Aristotle, was the founder of the physical sciences. Wilson
also acknowledges the pioneering work of Einstein, "the architect of
grand unification of physics, Ionian to the core" (5). But Wilson goes beyond both Holton and Einstein in at least two respects. First, he takes
as the scope of future convergence nothing less than all knowledge—not
just the sciences but also the social sciences and the humanities: "Nothing fundamental separates the course of human history from the course
of physical history" (9). Second, he envisions a coincidence of vision:
namely, that the convergence of all knowledge will in effect be a creation story, and tell us once and for all time who we are and why we are
here; and thus test and affirm perhaps Holy Writ, the science of mythol-
ogy. It will, in Wilson's view, constitute the 21st-century version of the
struggle for the soul.

What is particularly instructive about Wilson's views is his identification of what has or may continue to prevent or compromise convergence. Thus, socially and politically we are typically unbalanced: "the
vast majority of our political leaders are trained exclusively in the social
sciences and humanities; and have little or no knowledge of the natural
sciences" (1999, 13), and no one appears to be concerned about such a
lopsided and fragmented situation. Nor is it often any better on the
other side. There are physicists who do really not know what a gene is
and biologists who are ignorant of string theory. The "fragmentation of
expertise was further mirrored in the twentieth century by modernism

in the arts and architecture" (39). In short, pieces are being passed off routinely as wholes across the board.

Wilson offers a real-life illustration of typical fragmentation. Governments generally are having a difficult time developing a policy to manage dwindling forest preserves of the world. Clearly, this is a multifaceted problem. Minimally, it involves ecology, ethics, economics, and biology. Picture a quadrant in which each of these four fields inhabits one quarter of the quadrant. The fact that four perspectives are identified in the first place is a major step forward, but it deteriorates rapidly from this point on. Immediately, arguments of jurisdiction or territoriality surface. That is rapidly followed by the ego of size and extent: how big or small each of the quadrants should be. In the process, mutual ignorance comes to the fore. Each field knows little or nothing about the others but enough to challenge pretensions to the throne and their being in the arena or quadrant in the first place.

Let's change the configuration a bit, suggests Wilson. Draw a series of concentric circles of different sizes that cut across all the intersections of the quadrant. That establishes the agenda of consilience. The smallest circle would be a set of minimum interfaces that would permit each discipline at least to acknowledge both its contributions and their limitations. The larger, more inclusive circles stress connections rather than separations. The largest circle offers the collective, cumulative, and convergent. The higher one goes in the food chain, the bigger the bite.

But there are few established ethical guidelines, and those that exist generally are not shaped by ecological knowledge. The economics of sustainable yields is still a primitive art. What biologists know derives from short-term observations. The ecologists have been embarrassed by the boomerang of their premature death announcements as nature and animals often have bounded back. So there is a double problem: each discipline needs to deepen its own knowledge; and each discipline needs to know more about what they have in common with the others. Consilience compels the highest, most encompassing, and inclusive concentric circle that provides the optimum number of crossing and bridging points across boundaries.

It is Wilson's contention that when a convergence agenda becomes paramount, then increasingly the likelihood is that concentric circles rather than quadrants will be the primary structure. But the agenda needs to be shaped by the leaders of each discipline in order to guide the research throughout the entire enterprise. The politics of positioning may be necessary for the interfacing benefits to be realized in daily exchange.

There are, at least for Wilson, four great chasms that need to be bridged. They are C. P. Snow's notion of the conflict between the cultures of science and the humanities, the nature/nurture controversy, the physiology and psychology of the brain/mind, and the racial superiority/inferiority of world cultures. Not much progress has been made, because each side believes it is right and the other is wrong. According to Wilson, they are both right. Indeed, the most difficult conflicts to solve are not between right and wrong, but are conflicts of rights. Significantly, the way that Wilson seeks to bring about a more cooperative attitude and ultimately consensual convergence is in fact to reframe the opposition in terms that bring all the conflicts together under one roof

For example, the conflict between the two cultures is less the result of a fundamental antagonism than the creation of artificial territorial lines. If that were replaced by a "broader and mostly unexplored terrain inviting cooperative entry from both sides" (Wilson 1999, 126), a larger, more formidable, but more reconcilable version of the conflict would emerge. All human behavior and its artifacts are transmitted by culture. Biology has a share in the creation and transmission of culture: "The question remaining is how biology and culture interact, and in particular how do they interact across all societies to create the commonalties of human nature. What, in final analysis, joins the deep mostly genetic history of the species as a whole to the more recent cultural histories of its far-flung societies?" (126). Although Wilson admits that at the present time no one has the total solution, the answer already is apparent: "From diverse vantage points in biology, psychology and anthropology, they have conceived a process called gene-culture coevolution. In essence then, the conception observes, first, that to genetic evolution the human lineage has added the parallel track of culture evolution, and, second, that the two forms of evolution are linked" (127).

Similarly, the great divides between different human societies have nothing to do with race, religion, or the innate superiority or inferiority of certain peoples. It has to do with the chasm that separates scientific from prescientific cultures. Like Sowell (2005), Wilson accepts the notion that myth and religion function like science to explain who we are and why we are here. But without the knowledge of natural sciences, humans are trapped in a cognitive prison. Science, in contrast to art and religion, which seeks to preserve mysteries, penetrates mystery in order to demonstrate the incredible order of a world shaped by natural selection. Wilson brings the same logic to the nature/nurture controversy: both clearly are involved, and further genetic research on the one hand and in psychology and sociology on the other hand will produce more precise allocations of nurture or nature situationally and perhaps even individually. Finally, in this connection, Wilson believes radically that Freud needs to be suspended from providing critical explanations of dreams and unconscious behavior until sufficient empirical research has been conducted to verify or nullify his views. The causes and treatment of schizophrenia, which have eluded many psychologists, seem to be amenable more to a genetic explanation and appropriate psychological treatment.

Wilson is most tentative about the brain/mind duality. Like George Lakoff and Mark Johnson in their *Philosophy in the Flesh* (1999), Wilson starts with the basic premise that "natural selection built the brain to survive in the world and only incidentally to understand it at a depth greater than is needed to survive" (Wilson 1999, 61). Humans thus share with all other creatures the survival thrust of the brain. But to both master survival and achieve dominance at a higher level—in effect, to dominate the survival of all other creatures and the world of nature itself—the brain was compelled to create the mind. But that does not mean that the mind or the intelligence-gathering and analytical capacity of the mind was fundamentally different physically but rather neurophysically. In other words, the mind was still a scientific engine, not a soul or spirit. Indeed, current research needs to "to tighten the connectedness between the events and laws of nature and the physical basis of human thought processes" (1999, 65). The molecular biology of the learning process will considerably enhance the study and creation of artificial intelligence as well as the embryonic field of artificial emotion.

Finally, Wilson believes that the three great areas of inquiry and convergence for the next 20 years will be "mind, behavior, and ecology" (1999, 95). Equally as important is the recognition that the ultimate goal of all science is "predictive synthesis," still in its infancy but extremely important and attainable. It is not achievable without enough empirically based demonstrations of consilience. But the substantial development of such evidence will be the mergence of predictive synthesis as the ultimate fruit of convergence.

CONFLUENCE

What then are the yields of this examination of convergence as a megatrend? There are at least five. The most obvious is that convergence has the capacity to radically disturb not merely the branches but the roots of all knowledge. Second, it is developmentally progressive and supports an epistemological and structural taxonomy not unlike Maslow's classic hierarchy. The following stages of evolution appear basic:

1. Similarity
2. Duality
3. Parallel
4. Paradox/Ambiguity
5. Crossovers
6. Integration
7. Synthesis
8. Convergence, Connexity, Consilience

Third, convergence provides the theoretical and empirical basis for understanding and anticipating a number of developments born of integration. These include the technology of theology; the creation of an internal pharmacy, brain chips, and the third intelligence; the appearance of the great convergence (the fusion of science and spirituality); and the pursuit of immortality. Fourth, Mulgan took convergence into sociology, politics, and economics and envisioned interconnectedness as the antidote to excessive self-assertion by individuals and societies. His descriptions of the social benefits of connexity suggest that similar gains may be as possible and persuasive in the technological, scientific, and theological areas as well.

Finally, Edward O. Wilson offers resolutions to a number of the major debates of our time. In the process, he maintains that everything is linked, that nothing is singular, and ultimately that the physical, the spiritual, and cultural expressions of human existence and definition shall be known in common. It is a faith based on strong empirical research and documentation, and it represents his vision of the third millennium. But if it is to happen with less rancor, the specialists need to become generalists, and the generalists have to persuade the specialists to join them. The first step of convergence thus always requires exchange. The intermediate stage involves interdependence. The last step is always greater than the sum of all the crossovers.

REFERENCES

Burke, James. 1997. The great convergence. *Forbes* 22 (April).
———. 1995. *Connections*. New York: Little, Brown.
Clark, Kenneth. 1990. *Leonardo da Vinci*. Oxford: Oxford University Press.
Cochrane, Peter 1999. Carbon-silicone convergence. *Forbes* (August).
———. 1994. *Tips for time travelers*. New York: Macmillan.
Davies, Paul. 1994. *The last three minutes*. New York: Basic Books.
Douglas. M. 1974. *How institutions think*. New York: Harper & Row.
Faggin, F. 1997. Mind chips. *Forbes* 23 (May).
Feynman, Richard. 1998. *The meaning of it all*. Reading, Mass.: Perseus Books.
Gould, Stephen Jay. 1996. *Full house: The spread of excellence from Plato to Darwin*. New York: Three Rivers Press.
Guba, E. 1990. *The paradigm dialog*. Newbury Park, Calif.: Sage Press.
Helprin, Mark. 1999. *Variable patterns*. New York: Scribner's.
Hirsch, F. 1977. *The social limits of growth*. London: Routledge, Kegan and Paul.
Kurzweil, Ray. 1993. *The age of spiritual machines*. New York: Harper.
Lakoff, George, and Mark Johnson. 1999. *Philosophy in the flesh*. New York: Basic Books.
Mulgan, Geoff. 1997. *Connexity*. London: Chatto & Windus.
Nolan, R. L. 1995. *Creative destruction*. Cambridge, Mass.: Harvard University Press.
Romer, Paul. 2001. Post-scarcity prophet. *Reason Online*. Available from http://www.reason.com/0112/fe.rb.post.shtml (accessed 24 October 2005).

Schwartz, Gary, and Linda Russek. 1999. *The living energy universe.* Charlottesville, Va.: Hampton Roads.

Sowell, Thomas. 2005. *Black rednecks and White liberals.* San Francisco: Encounter Books.

Stacy, R. 1992. *Managing the unknowable.* San Francisco: Jossey-Bass.

Vogt, E. 1993. *Powerful questions.* Cambridge: MicroMentor Press.

Wilson, Edward O. 1999. *Consilience: The unity of knowledge.* New York: Knopf.

5

PUTTING FORECASTS ON TRIAL

A forecast should be tried by a judge and a jury, much like a criminal.
—*Future Trends* (Winter 2002)

In the wake of Enron et al., accountability and oversight increasingly are becoming new norms. For some it is too little, too late—and, more seriously, too alien. The controls are add-ons not organic to the process, Band-aids treating symptoms rather than causes. Besides, greed will likely be too creative and entrepreneurial to be content to replicate the old manipulations. But perhaps the most serious objection is questionable positioning. It is comparable to the old way of placing quality control at the end of the production line rather than as an integral part of the process at all key stages.

Would it not make more sense to be accountable beforehand and during rather than as an afterthought? And to be not outside but inside the process from the start, and thus be a more anticipatory and internally involved partner so as to avoid later embarrassing and panicky external correctives?

What are some of the essential characteristics and benefits of this more invasive and internalized concept of accountability? It should be proactive, participatory, and diverse (not one-size-fits-all); built into every major decision point and process; focused not only on pinpointing errors or lapses but also on improving the process itself; self-correcting; contributory to the larger process of continuous improvement; internalized, institutionalized, and integrated into each operation; and, finally, seamless.

How to start? Select initially those problem or fallible processes, structures, or roles. Then mercilessly put them on trial. Give each one the third degree, but make sure that the excess indicted is central and generic, not peripheral or occasional. Then and only then can accountability be built in as a self-correcting agent. To illustrate how it might work, putting forecasting on trial might be particularly appropriate.

FORECASTING

It has been argued that forecasting possesses so many flaws that it may not be amenable to any sort of accountability (Mintzberg 1994). In addition, the standard disagreements between strategic planners about theories, methodologies, and trend gathering have been around for some time now and no resolution seems in sight (Hamel and Prahalad 1994). Such a bewildering diversity of approaches may paralyze accountability by dispersing the crime over such an extensive area that one cannot take specific forecasts or the general process to task. But repositioning the focus may accommodate accountability (de Geus 1988). Specifically, to what extent have forecasts included assessing the capacity of the current workforce to realize such projections? More importantly, define the future workforce itself.

Already noted on an anticipatory and experimental basis are those companies that initially encouraged the crafting of employee mission statements (Buchen and Zdrodowski 2001). In addition, what has been called for is a gradual replacement of worker contracts with worker covenants (Champy 1999). Moreover, forecasts increasingly have focused on the transformation of jobs in both the short and mid-term (Habbel 2002). Most recently, Thomas W. Malone addressed the future of work (2004).

In short, a key means of holding forecasts accountable is to compel their addressing workforce trends and impacts constantly and comprehensively. Such a focus is both summative and precise. On the one hand, it encapsulates organizational mission, cultures, systems, and structures and renders them transparently operational. On the other hand, it captures the day-to-day drama, narrative, and cast of characters in the future in forms of scenario and simulation, the forecasters' version of science fiction.

The litmus test of futures accountability thus resides in its focus on workforce issues and its use as an insistent agent of reengineering (Hammer and Champy 1993). Finding weak data and trend links is to be followed by positioning accountability precisely at those points to correct the flaws, failures, and excesses from occurring in the first place. In addition, such checks and balances—when found, communicated, and put in place—stand a better chance of being self-correcting because they are intimate and proximate to basic and recurrent processes.

Sustaining and internalizing mock trials proactively might prevent real ones; requiring forecasts to endure the trial by fire of workforce projections and applications may forestall stillborn results. In short, any study that seeks the future range of business cannot do so until and unless it addresses the future of work and workers.

As noted at the outset, serious students of business have no other choice but to look down the road. It is also characteristically American. When at the end of the book it appears that Huck Finn might be taken in hand and finally civilized, he chooses instead to light out for the territory ahead. There, he, America, and its evolving workforce will remain forever young, resourceful, mischievous, and unfinished—like the future itself.

REFERENCES

Argyris, C. 1990. *Overcoming organizational defenses*. Needham, Mass.: Allyn & Bacon.

Bakken, B. 1993. *Dynamic decisions environments*. Ph.D. diss., Massachusetts Institute of Technology.

Buchen, I. 2002. Directive and nondirective employees. *PI* 44, no. 2 (May).

Buchen, I. 2001. Disturbing the future. *Foresight* 22, no. 4 (August).

Buchen, Irving, and P. Zdrodowski. 2001. Employee mission statements. *PI* 40, no. 6 (July).

Champy, James. 1999. *Reengineering management*. New York: HarperCollins.

de Geus. A. 1988. Planning as learning. *Harvard Business Review* (March/April).

Habbel, R. 2002. *The human factor*. New York: Booz, Allen, Hamilton.

Hamel, G., and C. K. Prahalad. 1994. *Competing for the future*. Boston, Mass.: Harvard Business School Press.

Hammer, Michael, and James Champy. 1993. *Reengineering the corporation: A manifesto for business revolution*. New York: HarperCollins.

Malone, Thomas. 2004. *The future of work: How the new order of business will shape your organization, your management style, and your life*. Boston, Mass.: Harvard Business School Press.

March, J. G. 1994. Decisions in organizations and theories of choices. In *Perspectives in organizational design*, edited by J. G. March. New York: Macmillan.

Mintzberg, H. 1994. *The rise and fall of strategic planning*. New York: Free Press.

Rosen, Robert, and Lisa Berger. 1992. *The healthy company: Eight strategies to develop people, productivity, and profits*. New York: Putnam.

6

OVERVIEW OF
FUTURE-DRIVEN APPLICATIONS

There are at least five major future-driven applications that already are operational: new training metrics, new strategic planning modes, corporate universities and their knowledge cultures, employee empowerment and productivity, and the future learning leaders—chief learning officers (CLOs).

NEW TRAINING METRICS

How have organizations and individuals coped with even the less exotic versions of flux? Basically, through three kinds of training and learning: catch up, line up, and cross over.

The thrust of catch up is incremental: bringing professionals up to date with the latest developments. These are usually add-ons. Occasionally, they may incorporate new directions, but in almost all cases they are focused and designed to bring everyone to the cutting edge or state of the art, together. Although future influenced, they are essentially present bound.

Line up involves structure, not content. It is also multidirectional and requires not so much the acquisition of new knowledge or skills as their constantly repositioning and prioritizing. The aim is to align individual and divisional goals with company objectives, especially if there are satellite centers, and especially if these are multinational. A key new learning complexity is managing and aligning multicultural and multigenerational diversity and values.

Crossover involves two kinds of additional learning. One is cross training. Coworkers are trained in each other's job not only for obvious purposes of replacement if necessary but, more importantly, to expand the knowledge and skills base of workers. The other crossover is more structurally ambitious—more interoperable. It involves linking the work focus of different divisions with each other to promote greater collaboration. It may link such operations as planning and customer service, marketing and auditing, purchasing and production, and so forth. Employees may spend a day or week, for example, on the phone in customer service. The goal is greater integration of function and process across the board.

NEW STRATEGIC PLANNING MODES

Because of increasing uncertainty and discontinuity, strategic forecasting needs futures thinking if it is to preserve its integrity as a discipline, on the one hand, and sustain the reality of its mid- and long-term projections on the other. The changes required reflect the degree to which the knowledge of at least three distinctive ways the future operates has been incorporated into strategic planning methodologies: in particular, patterns of escalation, degrees of knowability, and the partnership of monitoring.

Responding to future discontinuity varies with reaction time and with advanced intelligence. In fact, the goal of strategic planning is to preserve decision time and store options. But futures thinking, learning, and leading (FTLL) perceives unfolding prospects in the progressive and aggressive terms of stretch, strain, and shock. The sequence is ruled by a law of grim escalation. The first version of stretch, if ignored, is followed by the second, strain; and if that in turn elicits no response, then the third—shock—dominates the scene.

If the future is an enigma, it is a transparent one. It is an amalgam of the known, the unknown, and the unknowable. The obvious strategy is to move the knowledge base along that continuum. Extrapolation of present data and demographics builds the extent of the known in the present and the short term. Trending converts the unknown into knowable long-term patterns. But then all stops short with the unknowable, because that is, in fact, what defines the final future. But the consolation is that as much as two-thirds of what may come can be in hand.

Monitoring is no longer occasional and external but permanently embedded. It constitutes at least half of planning. Tracking sensors are distributed throughout to function as an early warning system to catch deviations. Monitoring requires its own plan. Usually it is a permanent overlay of data tracking equipped with its own software program, which has the capacity to adjust planning when certain parameters are exceeded or recalculated.

The futuristic adjustments of strategic planning produce not only a more integrated and dynamic whole, but also—and here again is the critical point—the plan itself would be a futures-thinking document. It would behave like the future.

CORPORATE UNIVERSITIES AND THEIR KNOWLEDGE CULTURES

The incredible growth of corporate universities, ranging from McDonald's to Ford to Disney to Toyota, bears witness to the centrality of training and learning as a major American and especially multinational investment in the future. Constantly responding to new challenges, corporate universities have been minimally involved in the process in two major future-oriented shifts: multinational acculturation and e-learning

Acculturating new employees whose work cultures are different and may in fact be at variance from that of the desired mainstream is an increasing focus of global companies. For example, Dell employs a number of software programmers from India and recently outsourced a significant portion of their customer tech support there.

Typically, employees from India favor supervisors who tell them what to do, and find it difficult to act on their own initiative. They prefer description to opportunity. Dell, which values worker participation over obedience and nonlinear thinking over rote learning, employs extensive situational training to bring about a shift in values and thereby a shift in work dynamics.

The other major change is the gradual conversion to e-learning. In some cases, a blended approach has been used for older, less technologically comfortable workers: traditional face-to-face classes have been joined with e-classes. The primary motivation is cost: lower instructional costs, less time away from work, elimination of travel and per diem expenses to centralized training sites, and so on. The other gain is increased quality control through standardization of content in the three areas noted above: catch up, line up, and cross over.

To a large extent, corporate universities are themselves future entities. They embody Senge's (1990) learning organization and incorporate Toffler's (1970) knowledge workers, which, when combined, create unique knowledge and learning cultures. They are almost like countries in their own right. To be sure, unlike traditional academic universities, corporate universities are ideological. They promote the perpetuation of their own survival and growth, and the bottom line. They are their own lobbyists. They, in effect, use themselves as case studies.

But individually and collectively, they also need to be corporate global citizens by including the new ideologies of global interdependence and sustainable development. It is not enough to hail and benefit from the global economy. It also requires the unique leadership of multinationals calling for and aspiring to world stewardship of the global commons. Such a commitment requires going beyond singular ideology to embracing an interdependent ideology that commands the international respect and loyalty of all professionals. In both instances, the value of futures thinking again is thus inevitably visionary.

Finally, futures thinking would encourage convergent thinking, which raises the integration of thought and process to optimum levels of synthesis without compromising differentiation. Whether or not the singularity occurs according to its projected timetable, what is clear is that it is born of and driven by convergence. Edward Wilson (1999) called it consilience to signify the future synergistic math of one plus one equaling three or four or five. Teilhard de Chardin (2001) claimed that "everything that rises converges." Discoveries or breakthroughs at the apex will in volcanic fashion reach out, touch, extend, and enrich all the other apexes to produce a total greater than the sum of its parts. In short, the visionary corrective here of the future itself is essentially a convergent force.

EMPLOYEE EMPOWERMENT AND PRODUCTIVITY

The obvious goal of training and learning is to increase the holy trinity of productivity, profitability, and quality. Of the three, the first enjoys the highest priority because of the competition of the global economy. To preserve their middle-class status, American workers have had to become more productive. Often, because of downsizing, productivity also involves fewer workers doing more. Although there are many ways of increasing worker productivity, one approach that has received generally less attention yet offers the option of a major application of futures learning and thinking is that of employee evaluation.

In the past five years, the nomenclature has changed. Employee evaluation has become performance evaluation and then shifted to its present version of performance improvement. Employees themselves have become human capital, and, as such, training is perceived as a way of securing return on investment (ROI). Worker agreements have in many organizations become worker contracts and finally worker covenants. The common denominator of all these changes is the increasing centrality of employee productivity and the increasing dependence of companies on the capacity of workers to constantly create or find cost-saving and creative ways of increasing productivity. There are signs that some organizations are contemplating a futures step in the performance improvement process.

Currently, the standard method to improve productivity is to encourage employees to consider how they might do their jobs differently. Many managers, especially those with seniority, have had to be retrained as coaches. They found it difficult to confer such initiatives upon the workers they supervise and to grant to those who do the job the expertise such that they know it better than anyone else. In some instances, the inquiry into performance improvement has been pushed further in two ways: asking employees to define and evaluate the effectiveness of the interfaces between divisions, and encouraging more overt interpersonal attitudes and behaviors so that receiving work satisfaction is accompanied by giving it as well to others.

The gains have been significant. Structural changes have been made, and interpersonal behavior modification has improved the mutuality of work environments. Matters appear to have gone as far as they can go, in the present—but not so, if one adds futures thinking/training.

The next logical step is to push inquiry into the future itself. Welcome though the changes recommended by employees on doing their jobs more productively may be, they are still present-bound. They deal with new configurations of various kinds, but they are generally incremental in nature. But endowing empowerment with more forward-looking vistas, workers can be invited to speculate on what they believe their jobs will be like in the future. Building upon their increasing competence in job review and change, workers not only may welcome such an opportunity but also warm to the task of projecting their future roles. Such worker projections can be followed by inquiring what kinds of training would be critical to get them from here to there. Such speculation can be a gradual rather than a one-shot process, and also may be accompanied by discussion and the distribution of some basic reading materials. In any case, the yields can be significant.

Individual projections of work change can be aggregated upward to generate patterns of the future that may shape that of the company itself. In addition, the same process may identify the common training needs and in effect identify the training agenda of the future. Of perhaps greater long-term importance, the process would contribute to developing a future-directed workforce. Finally, those companies supportive of such futures empowerment would have in effect created an employee-based alternative to the expert model in the form of futures learning communities. In all the above instances, the vision of the future not only brings a new dynamic to work environments but also shapes futures learning communities of best practices.

THE FUTURE LEARNING LEADERS: CHIEF LEARNING OFFICERS (CLOs)

One of the signs of the future arriving ahead of schedule is the emergence of jobs and titles for which there is often no previous classification or formal academic preparation. The positions of chief information officer (CIO) and chief learning officer (CLO) are cases in point.

No traditional or even corporate universities offer master's programs or degrees in learning management or have retrofitted existing executive educational programs to accommodate learning leadership at an executive level. And yet professionals are being appointed to such top-level positions, and a new journal (hard copy and online), professional organization, and website have appeared devoted to the CLO.

For many, the appearance of CIOs and CLOs comes out of the blue. Not so for futurists, but then they may be not only reenacting the emergence of futurists themselves decades ago but may also resemble their obsession with what is to come. Indeed, one can study and compile the emergence of every new profession as reflecting the regular and most current incarnation of the future.

CONCLUSIONS

Stepping back in order to sum up the arguments presented here on behalf of futures thinking, the first order of business may be to summarize them visually.

Futures Thinking and Learning Summary Matrix

Current Area Benefits/Outcomes	Futures Contribution	Future Changes
New Training Norms	Transition Training	Optimizing Knowledge
New Strategic Planning	Strategic Monitoring	Optimizing Choice
Corporate Universities	Global Interdependence	World Citizens
Employee Productivity	Future Work Projections	Future Workforce
Learning Management	Future Learning Foci	Future Intelligence

And similarly, perhaps the best way of expressing what futures thinking at different levels can bring to the learning challenges of the 21st century is to offer the following display.

**Progressive Components of Futures
Responses to Steep Learning Curves**

Futures Thinking	Divergent and Convergent
Futures Problem Solving	Innovation Methodologies
Futures Learning	Knowledge Anticipation
Futures Visioning	Paradigm Shift Anticipation
Futures Intelligence	Intuitive and Holistic Forethought

One final observation: Over the past two decades, a considerable amount of thoughtful work has been done in developing new theories of intelligence. One of the most impressive compilations is that of Howard Gardner, who in his 1983 book *Frames of Mind* identified seven kinds of intelligences. He subsequently added two more. To round the list out to an even ten, I would nominate futures intelligence as belonging to that list of essentials that, because of its convergent power, may exhibit the modest hubris of subsuming all the others.

REFERENCES

Gardner, Howard. 1983. *Frames of mind: The theory of multiple intelligences*. New York: Basic Books.

Senge, Peter M. 1990. *The fifth discipline: The art and practice of the learning organization*. New York: Doubleday/Currency.

Teilhard de Chardin, Pierre. 2001. *The divine milieu*. New York: Perennial. (Originally published in French in 1960.)

Toffler, Alvin. 1970. *Future shock*. New York: Random House.

Wilson, Edward O. 1999. *Consilience: The unity of knowledge*. New York: Knopf.

7

THE ANTICIPATORY SERVANT-LEADER

Robert K. Greenleaf, who has been hailed as the father of the empowerment movement, had two passionate causes: servant-leadership and the future. Although he is regarded as a lesser luminary among the better-known theorists and exponents of leadership, he sadly is also almost totally unacknowledged among writers and forecasters of the future as an anticipatory thinker. Although the reasons for this double neglect are not hard to find, they are instructive and may even pave the way for his greater recognition in both areas.

Unlike most students of leadership, Greenleaf is a Johnny-come-lately. He first began writing and lecturing and consulting on leadership only after he retired from nearly 40 years as an internal management consultant for AT&T. He wrote his first published seminal essay, "The Servant as Leader," when he was 73 years old. So Greenleaf appears to come out of nowhere, and he does so with his image of leadership totally at variance with the strong masculine notion of charismatic or transformational leadership. What intensified his acceptance, however, is that Greenleaf talked about institutions across the board—businesses, universities, seminaries, churches, foundations, and so on—and disconcerted everyone by attributing significant leadership leverage to boards of trustees, a group conspicuously absent from any discussions of leadership. But his call for the cultivation and emergence of an autonomous workforce did strike a powerful chord and led to his being perceived, at least in that area, as an anticipatory voice in the wilderness of human resources. Gradually, Greenleaf did secure the endorsement of respected leadership experts such as Max DePree, Stephen Covey, Joe Scanlon, and others, and the valiant efforts of the Greenleaf Center under Larry Spears did result in bringing to a wider audience the publications of Greenleaf's writings. Still, he is not where he should be. Ironically, that may be the fault of some of his more his enthusiastic endorsers, who predictably perhaps sought to assimilate Greenleaf into the mainstream of contemporary leadership thought.

Matters were probably worse as a futurist, for if Greenleaf had the unfortunate habit of surrounding leadership with a seminarian or academic halo unappealing to hard-nosed business professionals, his frequent references to the role of the biblical prophet and to the necessity for great dreams seemed a bit too romantic and starry-eyed for strategic planners and long-term projectors. But he knew what he was doing. Greenleaf was well-read; he knew what the favored leadership modes and mores were; he had evoked and even taught them in his many years at AT&T. So he also must have been aware that to call for CEOs to serve first and lead second would invite disbelief and even rejection. He also was also familiar with strategic planning at AT&T and long-range trend projections, too much so as not to be unaware that terms like prophets, seekers, and stewards would not endear him to those whose primary business was the future. So why did he come forth in clothes and words that clearly would not bring him favor or followers?

The answer is very simple and very Greenleafian. He saw things whole. He did not separate business from church from universities. They were all differently alike; they shared perhaps unknowingly some common big goals. They all did not just make money, educate the young, or save souls. They were all servants, even saviors, of civilization. In fact, Greenleaf's most powerful clinching argument for what he advocated is that precisely by becoming a servant-leader one can serve business, church, university, government agency, and, at the same time, civilization. Servant-leaders had access to totality. They did not separately or individually have to decide to be ethical or take the high road or develop a social conscience; it all came with being a servant-leader. Servant-leaders thus are always holistic. In his essay "Advice to Servants" (1975a), Greenleaf confesses that the "vast span of institutional life"— businesses, churches, universities, foundations—that he is addressing may jeopardize his credibility. But he argues for the "universality of the servant role," regardless of the complexity and diversity of the environments involved. The only lament that Greenleaf had was that servant-leaders from different institutions do not meet or talk to each other. If they did, they would confirm what he argues: the servant-leader is the archetypal leader.

Similarly, access to the future was also the sign of being a servant-leader. He witnessed what happened at AT&T when their vision, like a barrel without hoops, could not hold water and lost its containing power; and yet they clung to the past and refused to change even when things began to come apart. Greenleaf provides a capsule version of the prophetic role and process in his seminal essay "The Servant as Leader" (1973b) and especially in the subsection entitled "Foresight: The Central Ethic of Leadership." Greenleaf claims that every day of his life and at every moment of time the servant-leader has three simultaneous roles: historian, contemporary analyst, and prophet. These are not separate but continuous roles, just as the three time segments they respectively address (past, present, and future) are "bracketed and move along as the clock ticks" (2003, 53). The historian keeps alive the past and the long sweep of history. In a very real sense, the past is as big as the future. The most transient period of time is the present. To Greenleaf, the prophet has to know and acknowledge his roots in prophecy. He also needs to be aware of false prophets and those who see but do not act. It is not enough to look ahead but to look ahead with enough time and determination to do something about what is seen. Greenleaf cites Machiavelli's admonition: if one knows far off what evil is brewing, a cure is affected. "But when, for want of such knowledge, they [the evils] are allowed to grow so that everyone can recognize them, there is no remedy to be found" (53).

The present is the real world—busy, restless, and urgent. The contemporary analyst seeks the historical pattern underneath the fluxy surface, patterns of fragmented coherence, embryonic frameworks of the future. This analysis is not unlike that of Naisbitt in *Megatrends* (1982) when he claimed not to be describing the future but the present. It was not speculation about what might come; it was a narrative about what is going on right now. Peter Drucker (1998) echoed that practice in his article "The Future That Has Already Happened." But foresight is the most difficult role to understand and to practice.

Greenleaf confesses that foresight is a guessing game, although the prophet usually has a better-than-average record about what is going to happen and when. He employs the statistics of a moving average throughout time so that past and historical patterns and current events can serve as confirmatory or corrective or both. He also reduces risk by calculating future events and extrapolating from trend data. But inevitably one encounters information gaps. It is at this point that leaders who are determined to make foresight a totally rational process are fearful that without enough information they will make a major miscalculation, falter, and often fail. The way out is to borrow from the creative process and allow intuition to come to the rescue, as it invariably does to the leader open to the continuum of the past, present, and future. For those too self-possessed or narcissistic to abandon their dependence on rationality and to stay safely with conventional methods, Greenleaf's judgment is harsh: "The failure [or refusal] of a leader to foresee may be viewed as an ethical failure" (2003, 54). In fact, it is a double failure; it also involves the failure to be decisive when the freedom to act presents itself. Greenleaf concludes, "Foresight is the 'lead' that the leader has. Once leaders lose this lead and events start to force their hand, they are leaders in name only" (54).

The key role of the servant-leader then is to know the unknowable and to foresee the unforeseeable. That task unexpectedly is eased by fusing past, present, and future together and by making continuous the roles of historian, contemporary analyst, and prophet and their threefold determinations:

> Know Then
> Know Now
> Know Thence

As far as creditability is concerned, those who are leaders and prophets are to be believed and followed only if they are proven and trusted first as servants. Much of that trust derives from the fact that servants serve the future because no one can pretend to lead the future. The future resists such aggrandizement because the future is its own leader; it attracts its own followers. Even prophets are not leaders but rather articulators of the future; interestingly, Greenleaf claims that "prophetic voices of great clarity, and with a quality of insight equal to that of any age, are speaking cogently all the time" (1973b, 17). The variable that marks some periods as barren and others as rich "is the interest, the level of seeking, and the responsiveness of the hearers" (1973b, 18). Thus, not unlike followers who exist in a symbiotic and reciprocal relationship with leaders and fulfill the needs of both, responsive seekers bring to life and to fruition the leadership of prophecy and fuse past, present, and future. The constant antidote to presumption and excessive unilateral leadership is collaboration. Historians and contemporary analysts may not need supporters, but servant-leaders and prophets cannot exist without them—indeed, they flesh the word.

The discussion of Greenleaf as a futurist would be incomplete without another key concept and another way in which he may invite the uneasiness or even the suspicion of futurists. To Greenleaf, no speculation about the future can exclude vision and dreams, especially great visions and great dreams. He begins by examining what in fact visions do for us and how they have to be tested to determine whether they are true visions or not.

As Greenleaf describes the process, visions have a number of effects. First, they expand our vistas and open us up to bigness. They disturb in a lovely way our complacency. They are generally stirring. Second, they challenge what we know and think. They energize and focus our reflection. They invite processing and perhaps even premature assimilation. Third, they energize us to make the vision livable, to test its verisimilitude, to determine whether in fact it can live in this world with real people. Fourth, they force us to extract "hard reality" from a dream, not unlike Marianne Moore's famous paradoxical definition of poetry as an imaginary garden in which there is a real toad. Fifth and finally, the vision is acknowledged as the future. Thus, as noted, the future leads itself; the task is to make it available, to provide access so that the above process of benefits can accrue and so that sufficient time is provided to take curative action.

How does one know whether the vision or dream is true or false, just as how does one know whether a prophet is a true or a false one? Green-leaf has developed five tests of authenticity. The first has to do with the reality of the world that has to receive and accept it. The vision must be difficult to deliver. It must be resisted. It must be critiqued. If the vision encounters no obstacles, it is probably so obvious that there is nothing challenging about it or it rests on the assumption that everyone is perfect or an angel. Second, it must deal with the fundamental goodness of most of humankind, but it must be "rigorously benign." It cannot seek or expect a heaven on earth. That can't happen on earth, and to appeal to that vision is an appeal to the afterlife that cannot happen here. Third, it cannot shatter stability. It cannot be so discontinuous, revolutionary, or dramatically different from reality that it imprudently threatens the order of things. Greenleaf the historian reminds all visionaries that order is the first condition of all civilized societies, and they would sooner do without vision than do without order. Fourth, the vision must be persuasive, not coercive or manipulative. It should gather support gradually. Part of its authenticity is that it becomes a force for consensuality. Fifth and finally, the vision should address the two central dilemmas of the present and the future: alienation from society or work, and educating and maturing servant-leaders and institutions.

In summary, then, what are Greenleaf's central tenets as a futurist? The first is to commit oneself to know the unknowable, to foresee the unforeseeable, in short, to be anticipatory, to live in the future. This proactive role is the special preoccupation of the servant-leader whose task is in fact to serve the future and to be ahead and out there so that he or she can act ahead of things. Another key role is that of the contingency planner and thinker. This requires anticipating the unexpected and not being surprised into deflecting or abandoning the basic enervating and uplifting vision. But beware of utopian visions: "One cannot be hopeful . . . unless one accepts and believes that one can live productively in the world as it is—striving, violent, unjust as well as beautiful, caring and supportive. I hold that hope, thus defined, is absolutely essential to both sanity and wholeness of life" (1973b, 21). Finally, there is the discipline of foresight that seeks and endorses pragmatic prophecy, just as it itself rests on historical facts and creative intuition. The ultimate gift the future holds in store for its servant-leaders and those who listen and seek great visions and dreams is the continuation of civilization. Greenleaf is aware of the warnings of ancient prophetic voices: "It is the unexpected that most breaks a man's spirit" (Pericles), and "Without vision, the people perish" (Proverbs 29:18).

REFERENCES

Drucker, Peter. 1998. The future that has already happened. *The Futurist* 32, no. 8 (November).

Greenleaf, Robert K. 1973a. *The institution as servant*. Cambridge, Mass.: Center for Applied Studies.

———. 1973b. *The servant as leader*. Cambridge, Mass.: Center for Applied Studies.

———. 1975a. *Advice to servants*. Cambridge, Mass.: Center for Applied Studies.

———. 1975b. *Trustees as servants*. Cambridge, Mass.: Center for Applied Studies.

———. 1977. *Servant leadership: A journey into the nature of legitimate power and greatness*. New York: Paulist Press.

———. 1979. *Teacher as servant: A parable*. New York: Paulist Press.

———. 1980. *Servant: Retrospect and prospect*. Cambridge, Mass.: Center for Applied Studies.

———. 1998. *The power of servant-leadership: Essays*. San Francisco: Berrett-Koehler.

———. 2003. *The servant-leader within: A transformative path*. New York: Paulist Press.

Greenleaf, Robert K., Don M. Frick, and Larry C. Spears, eds. 1996. *On becoming a servant-leader*. San Francisco: Jossey-Bass.

Naisbitt, John. 1982. *Megatrends: Ten new directions transforming our lives*. New York: Warner Books.

PROACTIVE MANAGEMENT OF HUMAN CAPITAL

There have been many excellent studies and forecasts about the future of work, but such descriptions are often more symptomatic than causal. They may not reflect the deeper, more systemic changes transforming the workplace now and increasingly in the future at virtually all levels of employment. What may be helpful is to combine overview with long view and offer a dozen megatrends that are likely to drive and shape the future of work structures, environments, and personnel.

I. HORIZONTAL STRUCTURES

Many companies are changing their shape. Fewer have the look of the pyramid or a wedding cake. The thinning out of middle-level managers (AT&T), the integration of separate divisions along process rather than functional lines (Mitsubishi), and the outsourcing of many functions (General Motors) have shifted vertical alignment to horizontal extent. The net result is that the structure of organizations increasingly mirrors the dynamics of their operations. The way companies organize their work determines their look, not the other way around. They tend to be fluxier, more amorphous, and network-like. They resemble the geography of the European Union where movement between parts is made easier and more fluid. Organizations in turn will be more like a series of clusters or neighborhoods, more unfinished, more accommodating to add-ons and spin-offs. Above all, they will be more comfortable with the temporary and the transitional. But perhaps the most dramatic version of such horizontal fluidity is that it will accommodate changes at the top.

2. THE TEAM OF CHIEFS

Typically, organizations are led by CEOs. Often, when newly appointed, such chief executives clean house—replace existing senior staff with their own team. Indeed, that is why the media hound newly elected American presidents to reveal their appointments. The press knows how predictive they are in determining future policy. Increasingly, CEOs are surrounding themselves not just with senior staff but with other chief officers. The principals are the CFO (chief financial officer) and the COO (chief operations officer). Following horizontal directions, a new one has been added—the CLO (chief learning officer). This has been accompanied by a new professional magazine, society, and an online journal. (In Denmark, one CLO is designated as CIP—chief innovation pusher.)

Of course, the appearance of a CLO is an outgrowth of other, more established trends, especially that of Senge's (1990) learning organization. But more important it clinches both the new horizontal chain of command and the range of collaborative leadership. Increasingly, companies will be interviewing and hiring not just CEOs but executive leadership teams. Headhunters will favor prospective CEOs who have a group track record and who inspire and require their companion chiefs to be outstanding, loyal, and collaborative.

3. MOSAIC MULTIPLICITY

Currently, five demographic generations—soon to be six—coexist in a typically large company. That has been compounded by the mixture of races, religions, and ethnic cultures. Often such multiplicity is even invited and sought electronically. Many software developers use overseas programmers. Dell has exported and rerouted much of its customer tech service to India. But such diversity is not without its human resource (HR) difficulties. Harvey Swados (1957) pointed out a number of years ago that the friction between white and black workers on the automobile production line was not racial but related to work cultures. Most of the blacks had worked alone, not in groups, and so they were not familiar with the kind of "You scratch my back and I'll scratch yours" give-and-take work culture of assembly lines. Many of the programmers from India do not understand the American emphasis on individual initiative; they prefer assignment to opportunity. The work ethics of workers of different generations also often clash. The research shows that older workers prefer a more directive managerial style, while younger employees prefer a more indirect style. Typical Silicon Valley start-ups are single generational. As a result, they are more agile and fragile. They can move faster, but there is little internal tension from different generations to challenge the directions being taken. In short, the span and variability of the workforce has put a greater strain on HR and its acculturation and training agenda. The orientation of new employees has acquired a higher priority, and its duration has been extended from a few days or a week to yearlong. The rationale is protecting the investment in human capital.

4. HUMAN CAPITAL

Historically, capital was exclusively defined as financial in nature. Even inventory, stock, and market reputation and share were quantified. Some venerable institutions floated above the crass order of money and possessed a unique aura. Certain stock brokerage houses, insurance companies and banks, and Ivy League universities imparted cachet to their products and services. Not unlike the royal crown bestowed on certain firms, such organizations functioned as institutional dynasties. The professors at Harvard have a more programmatic than individual identity. It is the way the institution provides its value-added halo. But two major shifts made workers a more visible and assertive part of the equation.

Customer service and competition occupied center stage. The competition, especially from abroad, where workers were paid less, made productivity the driving issue; whenever that goal dominates, employees emerge as the key. They are the only equalizer. Companies who have achieved productivity gains each year ascribe it solely to employees, not managers, divisional heads, or even chief executives. And in this instance they were right to do so. In some cases, as at GE, worker gains are linked to productivity systems such as Six Sigma. The slogan became "Work smarter, not harder." Stephen Covey's (1989) fame rightly rested in great part on his admonition to sharpen the saw.

Increasingly, employees were designated as human capital to symbolize their new valued status, although that tribute was often belied and glaringly in conflict with the other force and focus of productivity, cutting costs by downsizing. But because the emphasis was on worker smarts and savvy, costs for training and tuition remission programs went from the millions to the billions. Corporate universities were created by Ford, Motorola, and McDonald. Deming's (1950) post-World War II statistical process control not only became more sophisticated and encompassing but also was designed to be used directly by employees themselves for corrective action. After all, it was the collective suggestion of employees that led Volvo to shift the location of its quality inspection team from the end of the production line and distribute it throughout the entire production line; within two weeks, the company celebrated its first day of no defects. Perhaps the crowning convergence is the merger of human capital and the knowledge worker.

5. CUSTOMER AS DATA

The commitment to customer service parallels that to employees. Two principal stages are discernible. The first stressed the obvious importance of customer satisfaction as a key source of repeat business. But marketing research went further and calculated the greater cost of recruiting a new customer against that of retaining existing ones. Loyalty programs like airlines frequent flyer programs and car purchases followed. Second, the customer increasingly became a data point. Buying patterns, adjusted by age and even ethnicity, were generated. Finally, customers were designated not as shareholders but stakeholders. As such, many companies formed customer councils (which often included vendors) to provide multiple perspectives: the perception of the quality of its products or services; the identification of customer-friendly divisions and employees empowered to go the extra mile; suggestions for improving productivity, profitability, and quality; and even the creation of new products and services. The elevation of the customer parallels the elevation of the employee. Both now enjoyed the status of partners.

6. THE TRAINING ABSOLUTE

Undoubtedly, what is behind the emergence of the role of chief learning officer is the convergence of three needs: smart employees; cost-effective, nondisruptive continuous improvement; and differentiated training programs. Smart employees need training to remain smart and to produce a constant and unbroken line of productivity gains. Traditionally, the training was largely incremental. New skills, new equipment, new software systems required regular and continuous updating. But increasingly employees were given stretch goals—goals that would often change and shift direction within weeks or even days after they were initially given. The training now had to include transition training and out-of-the-box thinking—how to mange flux and moving targets. Workers were introduced to the need to be agile and inventive, to think on their feet, and to develop quick solutions to fix not just one but many holes in the dike. Training became less conceptual and more situational. Crisis scenarios and exercises were presented in which survival was not assured. It was serious business; many did not make it.

In addition, training like everything else had to exhibit cost containment. That in turn meant that employees could not give up extensive time away from achieving their stretch goals. Nor could divisional budgets sustain the heavy expenses of traveling to and staying over two or three nights at a training site. Then, too, because of the different work values of many coexisting generations as well as the wide range of skill sets and cultural assumptions of a diverse workforce, training had to be differentiated, even individualized, to be effective. But the costs of constantly expanding training budgets had to be contained. Enter the chief learning officer. Solving those multiple problem became the task of CLOs. Their solution? Electronic delivery systems and differentiated software applications.

The changes were dramatic. The total number of programs was reduced to a fewer number, each with individualized subsets. Training via CD was portable and could be taken home or plugged in while traveling. Workers could proceed at their own pace. An extensive library of both in-house as well as outside links was made part of HR's homepage agenda for individual employee selection. Older workers who preferred the more traditional forms of instruction were wooed and weaned with blended instruction—classroom plus e-learning. The parameters of tuition remission programs were expanded to include advanced degrees from accredited online universities.

7. EMPLOYEE EVALUATION

Again, a name change signals future change. The first shift was that employee evaluation became performance evaluation. Like records of productivity, the focus shifted from observation to documentation, from description to data. Then stretch goals upped that to performance improvement. But again, to maximize and optimize the change, that required extensive alteration of the entire evaluation process and of the roles of managers and employees.

Evaluation had to be frequent and ongoing. It no longer could be a single-shot, annual occasion of a worker's anniversary. Multiple contacts changed the role of the manager to that of a coach. He had to develop a totally different supervisory style; in fact, it became the focus of his own evaluation.

As part of the evaluation process, employees were asked now to review and develop afresh their own job descriptions but recast in the form of job mission statements. The objectives were to encourage employees to take a more self-conscious and critical attitude toward their own work and how it was being done. That laid the foundation for asking the next key productivity question: if you could reconfigure the job so that it could be done differently, what would you change? And what would it take from other workers, including other divisions, for that job to be made even more productive? Tapping into the basic research that no one knows a job as well as the one who does it, the manager coach encouraged and practiced role reversal. The employee talked, and the manager listened, hearkened, and benchmarked the productivity goals of the new mission statements. To be sure, the law of scarcity dictates that authority can only come from a limited source. The steady rise in ascendancy of empowered employees has led to the general demise of middle-level managers whose future has become more precarious than ever before.

8. EMPLOYEE FORECASTING

Resourceful and enterprising companies and managers pushed the process further, even in spectacular fashion into the future. Mission statements were reviewed so that they were in synch with company objectives. That in turn often required that the components of the mission statement be prioritized to accommodate the all-important alignment. At the same time, employees were asked to push the learning envelope further and to speculate on how they thought their current job and mission statement would change in the future and, equally as important, what training it would take to prepare them for that future. Aside from assuring employees that the company planned to do everything it could to ensure their future, the training identified by employees basically shaped the future training agenda of the company. But perhaps the most ambitious and futuristic yield from this process was the addition of a forecasting overlay to job and training projections.

In a few companies, such as Fuji—admittedly high tech and thus always and routinely living ahead of its time—performance was fully extended to forecasting. Armed with books, articles, websites, and, above all, science fiction, different divisions of employees read, discussed, and speculated weekly on probable and possible future developments. The base always remained the familiar individual projections of each person's job. To be sure, that frequently underwent revision as it was nested within the larger big picture of the future, which gradually was taking shape through employee input. Compiled piece by piece and aggregated upward over a six-month period, what emerged was a series of common trends and directions on the future in general and on the specific futures of the company and each of its employees. Like the process of asking each employee to identify the training that would ensure his job in the future, this process offered the same ownership except now on a grander, more inclusive collaborative scale. In addition to providing material for strategic planning, it also served as grist for a Delphi mill. But whatever its subsequent use, what dramatically emerged was a new company priority and a new definition of human capital: a futurized workforce. The only question was degree. Companies would now be defined as to whether their employees were future-oriented, future-directed, or future-driven.

9. EMPLOYEES AS MANAGERS

Central to the above developments are a number of related and critical role-change trends having to do with managers and with the strong emergence of collaborative teams. Although it is not difficult to trace and to document the spectacular rise of middle-level managers, most are evidently reluctant now to acknowledge the trend of their gradual fall or demise. It all began with the thinning out of middle-level managers. Accustomed and equal to the task of reducing costs, many managers were surprised to find themselves the object of cost savings. Those who survived found their supervisory load greatly expanded, vacancies frozen or abolished, and their ability to manage a wide and diverse range of employees—many of whom lacked even the most basic skills set—strained. Inevitably, slippage of various kinds occurred, and productivity targets were not met. Then came the next blow. Managers were asked to group workers and to coach them into high-performance teams. Then with the paranoia of a suicide, they were finally asked to step aside and allow the team to choose its own leader from within its own ranks and to run itself. Mangers increasingly became marginal. They came to resemble those displaced intellectuals in a Chekhov play who walk around wailing, "I am a superfluous man; I am a superfluous man."

As performance evaluation became both group and individual, collaboration not only enjoyed a new centrality but also required a new definition of job satisfaction, which now included providing job satisfaction to others. The new team of human capital required in turn a new codification of their team relationships. What gradually emerged was tantamount to a new definition of the social contract: the notion of the work covenant (as advanced by Hammer and Champy, 1993). To some extent, it served to provide the badly needed glue of coherence to replace the damaged and battered notion of company loyalty. Now it was given intimate and real proximity in and within the team. The group would accomplish and protect what was beyond the individual capacity of its members. Even the role of team leader was defined in an egalitarian way—he or she was at best *primus inter pares*—first among equals. Moreover, the position of leader was temporary and rotational. If the problem faced required a different kind of expertise, then the one who possessed that expertise became the team leader. Above all, teams were required to be self-organizing, self-planning, and self-managing. In short, it reflected the emergence of employees as managers. To be sure, such appropriations of power and authority could only come from areas of authority ceded by management and even executives.

10. DISTRIBUTED LEADERSHIP

Just as employee managers would not be conceivable without understanding the changes in middle-level management, and without the new coherence of mission statements and worker covenants, so the related shifts in leadership redefinition require a bit of developmental history. Two seminal thinkers fused here for convenience need to be explored—Robert K. Greenleaf and Charles Handy.

Greenleaf and Handy favored executives who served the organization rather than the other way round, who were committed to developing and empowering everyone they touched, and who finally recognized that leaders and managers do not have a monopoly on leadership. Both Greenleaf and Handy were not content for employees to be merely managers; they wanted them to be leaders as well. In fact, as a consultant, Handy persuaded a number of his client companies to have employees write leadership options into their job descriptions. Ritz Carlton pushed it further by empowering every employee, including chambermaids, to do whatever it takes including going way beyond customary responsibilities to solve customer problems. In the Fasson plant in Indiana, team leaders are given credit cards with an upper limit of $10,000 to order replacement parts for a production line that is down. In the experimental charter schools of Ed/Visions of Minnesota, teachers collectively run the school and there is no principal. In short, leadership no longer was exclusively focused on or limited to the top. It now became distributed. The key was to persuade executives that the ultimate expression of their leadership was to share it. No CEO, no matter how transformational and charismatic, could match the 360-degree range of diffused leadership.

11. INTERNALIZED AND SELF-CORRECTING MECHANISMS

The overriding pattern of all the above trends has been that of recasting, refining, and redistribution. The same deck of cards is still essentially being used. The players may have changed, the stakes clearly are higher and tougher, but the winners are still those who know how to play the old game in a futuristic way. The key to the future then is not so much introducing the new as reorganizing the old. Nothing perhaps dramatizes that claim more forcefully than the issues of accountability and of futurizing organizations.

The characteristic impulse is add-ons. Close the existing loopholes, tighten and expand the rules and regs, appoint oversight committees like U-2 spy planes, and all will be solved. Similarly, futurize an organization by importing outsourced forecasts and consultants, hire a resident or visiting futurist as an executive coach, and develop an elaborate series of electronic links for strategic planning. The problem with such external overlays is that the gains tend to be minimal, additive, and temporary. They are not integrated and wired in place and made a permanent part of existing systems. Above all, they are external to the organization. They do not affect or change it from within. They constantly require more input in an addictive fashion. Worst of all, they function as permanent scaffolding, never to be removed once the building is complete.

For accountability to work it must be built into all basic operations as a self-correcting check-and-balance mechanism. That is the only way to outguess and outmaneuver future clever attempts at evasion. The only way for an organization to become future directed or driven is to build proactivity into everyday processes and functions. It must

be hard-wired in place. It has to reapportion leadership, recast
employee evaluations, and even change the nature of empowering
conversations. That does not happen easily or quickly. The guideline
of such internal rearrangements is the permanent partnership
between the participatory and the anticipatory. One cannot have one
without the other. Quick and dirty external fixes will not take or last.
And the old magic of the solitary leader as a spellbinder no longer
carries the day.

12. FUTURE RESOURCES OF HUMAN RESOURCES

HR and its new ally at the top, the CLO, have to become advocates of
the new governance structures and leadership options of the future.
Only HR has the inside positioning and training track record to negotiate internal and comprehensive forward-looking changes in relationships and structures and to have access to a ever-increasing research
base of best practices to make a difference. In many ways, the future directions of all current reorganizations rest with HR and the correlations
between management style and learning styles, and between new
worker covenants and organizations redefined as communities not com-
modities. It short, HR has to live up to its name and offer futures that
are both humane and resourceful. If it succeeds, then human resources
will become a futures resource in its own right.

REFERENCES

Covey, Stephen R. 1989. *The 7 habits of highly effective people*. New York: Si-
    mon & Schuster.
Deming, W. E. 1986. *Out of the crisis*. Cambridge, Mass.: Center for Applied
    Studies.
———. 1950. *Some theory of sampling*. New York: Wiley.
Greenleaf, Robert K. 1973. *The servant as leader*. Cambridge, Mass.: Center
    for Applied Studies.
———. 1975. *Advice to servants*. Cambridge, Mass.: Center for Applied Studies.
———. 2003. *The servant-leader within: A transformative path*. New York:
    Paulist Press.

Hammer, Michael, and James Champy. 1993. *Reengineering the corporation: A manifesto for business revolution*. New York: HarperCollins.

Handy, Charles. 2002. *The elephant and the flea: Reflections of a reluctant capitalist*. Boston, Mass.: Harvard Business School Press.

Senge, Peter M. 1990. *The fifth discipline: The art and practice of the learning organization*. New York: Doubleday/Currency.

Swados, Harvey. 1957. *On the line*. Boston, Mass.: Little, Brown.

9

CHIEF LEARNING OFFICERS AS LEADERS OF UNIVERSITIES: REDUNDANT? OR RENEWING?

Why would a university, of all places, need a chief learning officer? Isn't that like bringing coals to Newcastle? Or disciples to MIT? Are not all or most professors CLOs? But looking more closely and especially from the inside, there are at least three reasons and benefits.

The first and most obvious is the need to prepare students for future roles and careers. Accounting programs long ago focused on the role of the CFO and identified the educational requirements for that top executive position. A small number of enterprising programs featured the specific dynamics of the CFO in an equal and shared relationship with the CEO, which turned out to be prophetic alliance for many companies, especially in the wake of post-Enron reconfigurations. In addition, a few academics recently have taken a leaf from (surprisingly) the field of education and moved in the direction of creating accountability standards for both CEOs and CFOs. Expanding that model to be more inclusive of disciplinary crossover, integration, and convergence would create a more horizontal version of future career directions. In fact, it might do well to develop an interdisciplinary curriculum for training learning leaders. What would it include? What connections should it have to other curricula? And who would teach it?

The second benefit is that a university-based CLO would challenge faculty and curricula status quo. Unlike a vice president of academic affairs, a dean, or a department chair who is usually absorbed in daily operations anyhow, a CLO would function as an independent, autonomous, and intellectual ombudsman. Those outside the academy may not fully appreciate its capacity for inertia. Less than one-fifth of all faculties engage in research. The working bibliography of almost all the rest bears the date of when they secured their terminal degree. In addition to challenging the faculty, the CLO would challenge existing curricula.

But why should that be questioned? For one thing, as already noted, current curricula are not future driven. Many courses do not reflect the basic changes, urgent trends, and new directions of current business operations, structures, and leadership. Indeed, undergraduate business requirements typically are such a mirror match of those for the MBA and even the PhD that the student is basically involved in duplicative rather than differentiated development. But to demonstrate the potential impact a CLO at a university might have on both faculty and curricula, the example of the human resources field will suffice, especially since human resources is a likely source from which future CLOs may arrive.

HR is undergoing a crisis. Its training budgets generally have been decimated; many of its functions have been outsourced (including sadly, and most recently, 360-degree evaluation); recruiting, interviewing, and orienting of new hires often have been parceled out internally and in the process bypassed HR; and e-learning often has been implemented as a training quick fix or overlay without being accompanied by a follow-up and monitoring system. And on top of all that, along comes the proposal to appoint a CLO, a rescuer who sadly may not be able to save the falling House of Usher.

Who puts Humpty Dumpty back together again? Same or new shape? What is the glue? Given the current fragmentation of HR, faculty need to question the basic assumptions of the field and review and redesign the entire curriculum. One of the unabashed goals should be to reclaim lost ground and prominence, but not by dressing up or hyping the old with e-learning and public relations. Rather, integration has to become the new driving norm and source of coherence. Employee evaluation, goals alignment, and professional development have to become seamless. Employee empowerment has to be ratcheted up to include employee mission statements, self-gap analysis, and personal and organizational forecasting. Above all, faculty have to focus on the future sources of human resources, which will offer CLOs access to the total range of trends, not just those affecting HR. In short, the task of an academic CLO is to bring the university boldly into the 21st century and beyond. A new HR curriculum would be a critical way to start.

Although the third benefit ideally is folded into the second, it is too important and often unacknowledged not to be separately identified and discussed. It involves the involvement and empowerment (not unlike that of employees) of adult graduate learners in curriculum development. In effect, they would be the strongest allies, even versions, of the CLO. They would provide the faculty with a reality check. They are directly anchored in current operations and pressures, place a high value on problem solving, and are adept at translating academic and intellectual concepts into best practices. In short, they would be invaluable partners in the curriculum redesign of HR. If a new program to prepare CLOs were also in place, many would qualify and apply, spurred perhaps by the challenge of the partnership with faculty and each other.

Cynically but accurately, comprehensive opposition of faculty and even administration to a having a CLO would be the best case for having one. The value attached by the academy to being protectively insulated from political machinations or the marketplace is often overstated and precious. Moreover, such disengagement is frequently violated on both sides. Obviously, employed graduate students, often on tuition remission programs, routinely and happily bridge the gulf between work and study and often challenge the intellectual constructs that reinforce such gaps. In effect, each student is a case study. Then, too, some of the best business and HR faculty are active consultants who are constantly pouring new wine into the old wine skins. When very successful, they often buy out their contracts on an annual basis and write best sellers that are really recreated consulting experiences laced with academic citations. In any case, the loss of such scholar practitioners deprives the university of a model for students and shifts the interactive exchange between student and teacher to the unilateral distillations of a best seller.

The strongest advocates for a university CLO are those who have been stretched by students; are aware of academic inertia, myopia, and opacity; and have worked alongside HR personnel going up a down escalator. Moreover, given all the reengineering that would have to be done, and the predictable turf wars of faculty and administration, perhaps only the senior-level position of a CLO would have the clout and leverage to bring about the learning of change. Of course, the embattled CLO would have at least three allies: students, alumni, and employers, and perhaps a fourth: corporate universities.

10

TRANSITION TRAINING
AS FUTURE TRAINING

The standard expectation is that dislocation is both temporary and non-recurrent. It is a singular event that happens infrequently; if one is just patient, everything will return to the way it was. After all, everything follows a regular cycle of ups and downs. But suppose the transition lasts a very long time, much longer than previous transitions have done. Or worse, suppose that the transition finally gives way not to reassuring and familiar stability but to another transition. And suppose further that the transition is replaced by another and still another; and so on and so on. What then? When that happens often enough, and embraces many different sectors, then transition and not stability becomes the norm—then we confront the paradox of continuous discontinuity. The only problem is that we have not been trained to accept transition as a permanent and recurrent reality. Instead, we have worshipped the absolute god of stability.

But what if one were to acquire another outlook entirely, to perceive transition not as the exception but the rule? With such expectations, we would not have to develop a forecast that is surprise-free. Surprise would rise every day with the sun. Rather than avoiding change or running away from threats of novelty, we would regard them as daily occurrences; we might even welcome them with a new expectation as the constant of reality.

There is a need for transition training, especially of teams. Groups tend to be both resistant and inventive. In many ways it would be like transition insurance, which a company might take out to protect its investment. What would such training consist of? Fortunately, we do not have to reinvent the wheel. A great deal of experience and research already has been done in another field and sector, which may be transferable. The education and survival of students in international settings has involved extensive exposure to transition techniques that have successfully negotiated the emergence of just the sort of flexible assumptions that we seek. It is also appropriate perhaps that business sit back and be lectured by education rather than always the other way around.

Many young students who are the children of governmental officials, the military, business executives, and so on are forced to leave their native culture, language, and environment for one that is foreign in many senses of the term. International private schools are like miniature versions of the United Nations, enrolling students from many different countries with value systems that may be obviously and subtly in conflict with each other. Obviously, the key concern of the school is how to address the problem of transitional culture shock for students. For business, the focus is not much different: how to help managers add to their expertise by learning how to manage transition. Here in summary form is what international schools have found to be the principal psychological signs of transition syndrome.

There are three basic symptoms of transitional shock that appear with escalating intensity. Each one is paralleled with an appropriate match in business management.

ANXIETY

Behaviors

Students and managers are nervous and unsure of themselves. They are not as confident about their tried-and-tested skills of coping. They are more suspicious than usual. They tend to keep to themselves. They become quiet, adopting a wait-and-see attitude. They expect the other shoe to drop at any time. Everything other than the most routine tasks is put on hold.

Outcomes

Transition exacts its price in reduced work flow and decision avoidance. Much becomes tentative. Reports are incomplete, and problem solving is clumsy or timid.

Relationships are limited to minimum exchanges. Students and managers walk around self-contained and sealed unto themselves. Talk is steely and minimalist. There is no joking or horsing around.

Conditions

Transition has created a generally nonproductive environment ruled by tentativeness. This is not unlike the situation in which a new headmaster or CEO is announced and subsequently described as a change agent. In business it also resembles rumors of mergers, downsizings, IPOs, sell-offs of divisions, and the like. The primary fear is that the outcome and the future are uncertain, and that whatever is going on hopefully will not last much longer.

DISCOMFORT AND DISORIENTATION

Behaviors

But the situation persists, as the law of escalation takes hold and ups the ante. Uneasiness is replaced by confusion. The student and the manager are constantly puzzled. They do not understand or respect the behaviors of those around them. They are particularly confused by two groups—the happy-go-lucky cohort who is often almost giddy and the others who walk around like automatons or robots. They feel increasingly isolated.

Outcomes

The situation is not unlike the survival simulation exercises companies use to determine ability to work in teams. In fact, many teams do not make it and perish. So, here, many begin to doubt their ability to survive. Students are busy writing letters to their friends or making phone calls. Managers are looking at the classified ads. Neither is comfortable or desperate enough yet to talk to parents or spouses.

Conditions

Increasingly, there is the recognition that something is basically wrong, and the solution, if there is one, is beyond the ability of a single individual. Something collective and institutional must be done to set the ship of state back on keel. This is the first time that the student and the manager turn away from inward self-doubt to outward accusation. There is an angry call for remediation.

ANALYSIS: DATA PATTERNS

Behaviors

Individually but especially collectively, students and managers begin to pool their knowledge. They begin by creating a common database of what they do not know. They note that the rules seem to have changed. In fact, they conclude that the game itself has been altered, that there is a new set of hierarchical values, and that these new values represent the outcomes and laws of their new environment.

Outcomes

Uncertainty has replaced certainty. Nothing is predictable. There is no relief in sight. The scale of the change is incredible; it is total. The pace is not occasional but continual, constant, and relentless. It is a science fiction experience and world.

Strategies

No one has any answers. The CEO and senior mangers do not know any more than the rank and file. Transition has leveled the hierarchies of the organizational chart. Leadership is now up for grabs. If there is a way out, groups (not CEOs) will muddle their way through.

But at least three guidelines and strategies are clear. First, traditional sources of stability have to be let go, perhaps even forgotten. Grieving should be short and final. Second, assumptions and expectations have to be generated by the new reality with the understanding that they may not last. They are like scaffolding that is never taken down because the building may have to change or be rebuilt. Third, creativity or innovation may have to replace or transform into analysis as the way out. Indeed, ultimately, many may become grateful that transition has come along as a form of birth and liberation.

The students who survive transitional culture shock are sturdier, more stable and creative students who live and breathe change. They are now at home everywhere they go in the world. In fact, it might not be an exaggeration to describe them as global citizens, not just comfortable but flourishing in diversity, not just surviving but growing on transition, not just prepared to meet the future but a different, even unpredictable future. And what of their adult counterparts? What profile of transitional managers would emerge? What would be their differences from traditional managers?

Traditional Managers	Transitional Managers
Managers of past patterns	Managers of flux
Top-down and singular knowledge base	Collaborative and evolving base
Linear-sequential planning	Circular and contingent
Exclusivity	Inclusivity
Concentrated	Distributed
Restructuring	Reengineering
Analysis	Intuition and innovation
Assumptions of continuity	Expectations of discontinuity

Although no one would normally seek the anxiety, dislocation, and disorientation of prolonged or frequent transitions, most companies and schools would be better managed and steered through turbulent and discontinuous times with managers of transition than with managers of tradition. Indeed, perhaps if the entire process of education and training had started earlier with international schools producing global citizens of transition, then that would be where companies could look for their future CEOs and managers.

ANTICIPATORY PERFORMANCE REVIEW

All performance reviews are retrospective. They typically look back to what was done or not done, well or poorly. If the process is enlightened enough to use coaching rather than judging, then dialogue is often invited between supervisor and employee: "If you had it to do all over again, what would you do differently?" Such an exchange when deftly coached often increases motivation, ownership, and performance. But still the focus is on the past, not the future. It is a way of improving what was, not anticipating what will be. Human resource professionals have the opportunity to play a pivotal role in pushing the envelope further—in transforming performance review into an anticipatory process and even a forecasting tool, in supplementing retrospect with prospect. Yet the basic questions that need to be answered first are: Why do it? What benefits will accrue?

BENEFITS OF ANTICIPATORY PERFORMANCE REVIEW

The most obvious advantage is that an anticipatory performance review (APR) accommodates the increasing practice of raising the bar of performance. It is not unusual to find employees facing as many as three incremental challenges or goal changes in one year. This is compounded in situations where there has been downsizing or cutbacks and where more employees are routinely expected to do more than they ever have before. Many organizations have already introduced what they call "stretch goals." What an anticipatory performance review may do is structure stretch competence to at least provide employees with the tools to manage what is now increasingly expected of them. Thus, for example, if a change in goals is likely to occur over the next year, the strategy that might be discussed and negotiated is how gradually to anticipate meeting those goals, or selecting the final most ambitious goal and set that as the task for the year. As Pericles noted centuries ago, "It is the unexpected that breaks man's spirit." Surprise can be demoralizing because it is accompanied by the expectation that there will never be an end to upping the ante. At least getting a hold on that future, and in effect managing change, offers a fighting chance to grow to the challenge.

The second benefit is diagnostic. Anticipating what is to come prepares for the key questions: How well prepared are we for that change? What training do we need? What special skills should we be looking for in new hires? Such key questions are short-term on the one hand and anticipatory on the other. They help human resource personnel to develop two key plans: a training schedule and succession or replacement plan.

The third benefit is innovative. It involves factoring into performance review the benefits of training. It thus attempts to find a way of measuring not the training but its implementation. The obvious value is to provide feedback to trainers on the one hand and to justify the funds expended for training on the other hand. In addition, it introduces the key concept of measuring growth and the response to change as part of performance review and improvement. As such, it supports career development planning; and where bonuses or gain-sharing plans operate, it provides a systematic and reasonably objective way of making those judgments.

These significant benefits can be facilitated by introducing (especially in a coaching environment) a number of key discussions between supervisor and employee. A considerable portion of the dialogue is generic in nature and can be shared with a group as a whole by the supervisor alone or with a partner from HR. That is to be followed by individual conversations in which the employee and the supervisor develop a specific match or link to that employee's job and key job parts and standards. Minimally, three structured dialogues, outlined below, will help conceptualize and anchor the benefits of implementing an anticipatory performance review.

The first conversation has to do with goals, in particular changing goals, stretch goals, and futurized goals—in short, the entire prospect of job change. Workers generally resist having their targets and tasks redefined. This is often true for employees who have a strong sense of achievement and order. One approach is the big picture—what is going on globally in the business and in the industry. Employees, especially those with a number of years with the company and who have survived a number of CEOs and changes in senior management, are remarkably interested in the subject and have many good and intelligent suggestions to offer. That has to be linked to business objectives (which, in turn, finally have to be linked to each of their specific goals and tasks).

Goals tend to be generic. There are basically five: productivity, profitability, quality, customer satisfaction, and empowerment. The process of futurizing involves the dynamics of the three following I's: increase, improve, innovate. For example, if one of the stretch goals is to increase productivity, the issue for discussion is how do we meet the new targets? But for effective problem solving, the other two options should also be considered. Thus, if the new target is not reachable just by incrementally upping the effort, then the discussion becomes how we can we improve or alter the process so as to become more productive. Suppose also we begin to face the limits of productivity; can we come up with a totally innovative way of accomplishing the task that is perhaps unique to the industry?

This kind of exchange can be applied to any of the business goals and involves the use of problem-solving dialogue but now applies to future goals and challenges. Individual discussion brings the issue home to its applications in terms of key job parts and performance measures, except now these are projected into the future. The other piece that is phased in at this point is support to accomplish goals. What training is needed in order for employees in a particular unit to accomplish their new stretch goals? And what kind of support—computer, personnel, budget, and so on—would be helpful to facilitate that accomplishment? To ensure that the actions being contemplated are precise and measurable for the next time around and to structure the evaluation of change and growth, the training should be described in terms of competency outcomes. In other words, rather than designating a workshop on problem solving and innovation, for example, it would be better to describe such core competencies as thinking outside the box, reconceptualizing the situation, unlearning, and so forth; it should be made clear that these will be measured in the future as the training is implemented and applied to each individual. In effect, the company will be able to measure, perhaps for the first time, the capacity of its employees to grow and to learn. That in itself will be a form of future insurance.

Another critical dialogue still focused on achieving business goals has to do with human dynamics—that is, people-to-people relationships. When Motorola wished to shorten the time between a customer's first placing an order and when the order is delivered, they discovered that whatever gains could be achieved within a unit, twice that number was achieved in the relations between units. In other words, in this case, as in many others, performance is relationships. But what helps to maximize or, better still, optimize relationships? There are at least three demonstrated ways employees significantly can improve their working relationships and therefore their productivity. And again using the question-and-answer method of dialogue rather than the directive and often preachy approach, three dialogue subjects can be introduced: the collective, the cooperative, the collaborative.

The collective is the familiar notion that everyone is important and, in different ways, contributes to the success or failure of the company. For this to have real meaning, however, the linkage between an individual's key job parts and performance standards and the organization's objectives has to be clear and firm. In fact, aligning individual and group performance with the overall goals and mission of the organization has become such a key managerial responsibility that it often determines the outcome of their own performance review. In the spirit of stretch goals and stretch competence, once the collective attitude has been inculcated, the next step is to discuss the cooperative mode, especially one that involves cross-training. Here the emphasis ideally shifts from the "me" to the "we," from the individual to the group unit. A quick test of that cooperative culture taking hold occurs when a member of the unit is ill and the rest get together to solve how they collectively and cooperatively will take up the slack and get both that job as well as their own jobs done. Finally, there is the collaborative mode, which is the glue that holds teams together and brings the collective and the cooperative to their highest fulfillment. The ultimate test of the collaborative is when the team is given the opportunity to hire, train, and fire and there is virtually no turnover of personnel; the team becomes in effect a miniature of the whole—a company within a company.

One other option involves a more radical commitment to future thinking and planning, and that involves having the cooperative and/or collaborative group collectively involved in a future scanning process. The goal is to bind employees permanently to a futures orientation by having them identify and develop through readings and weekly discussions the trends that will affect their company, their industry, and even their own jobs. The trends identified are even ranked by the group as to the degree of probability and impact. As the trends are aggregated upward, common themes are discovered, and the entire monthly process feeds into the strategic planning process. It is a highly professional way of becoming a futures-driven company and at the same time creating a high-performing culture.

One last benefit: with such an anticipatory performance review process in place, senior management in effect is provided uniquely with a human resources forecasting tool. They would know, for example, the capacity of their employees to accomplish the stretch goals that have been promulgated, be able to assess how much further those goals can be pushed, be aware of the training required to support performance improvement, and reap the benefits of a company culture that places a high value on the collective, the cooperative, and the collaborative. Above all, they would witness the gradual evolution of a company from one that is futures oriented to one that is future directed to ultimately one that is future driven. In the process, many employees would be persuaded that the company and they have a future—collectively, cooperatively, and collaboratively—together.

(12)

FUTURE MANAGEMENT METAMORPHOSIS: EMPLOYEES AS MANAGERS

There are various ways of measuring the vitality of any business component (Argyris and Schön 1974). What does it contribute, how decisively, with what reverberating impacts? Does it comfortably straddle and converge financials ranging from return on investment to the bottom line? Does it worship the holy trinity of productivity, profitability, and quality? Is it often the minion and advocate of HR? In short, is it indispensable? Earlier, the answer for management would be an easy yes to all of the above. Not so lately, and currently.

We know what has brought about the rise but not the decline (Champy 1999). The first and still the most telling blow to indispensability was the thinning out of the ranks. Accustomed to containing costs by reduction in force, mangers suddenly found themselves viewed as cost factors. Their role shifted from being the subjects to being the objects of fiscally directed decisions. Those who were left behind had to take up the slack and supervise a greater number of employees. Inevitably, slippage occurred—evaluations were occasional or perfunctory; orientations of new workers were cursory or delegated; the game changed from keeping up to catch-up; supervision had to focus on the most fundamental levels working with employees who did not possess the basic skills sets. In short, managers had to manage more, and more with less.

But then the second blow came. Employees had to be put into groups (Buchen 2000). The manager became not a leader but a manager of teams. He or she had to settle squabbles over turf and values, allow regularly for petty and self-indulgent venting, and negotiate consensus, which took the form of agreement by exhaustion. And then just when the teams were beginning to shape up, along came the cruelest cut of all: the teams were to be self-managing, self-organizing, and ultimately self-supervising. The team leader at best was *primus inter pares*—first among equals—and was to be selected from within the ranks (Greenleaf 1977). In some organizations, the teams aggressively pushed for more and more authority: they wanted to do their own hiring, they wanted greater autonomy of problem solving, and, in some plants, team leaders were given credit cards with a $10,000 line of credit. In less than a generation, many middle-level managers went from being indispensable to being marginal, from being central to being peripheral.

Interestingly, the same thing was occurring elsewhere, in education of all places, which routinely has never been emulated as a business model. A case in point is the emergence of the teacher as both a learning manager and as a learning leader (Lambert 2003). The former is a generic, across-the-board development applicable to all teachers. The latter applies to learning leaders who replace principals or supervisors but remain in the classroom. In other words, if education is displaying an anticipatory trend, then the next stage of the evolution of management may be the passing the baton and transferring the mantle of leadership to employees altogether. If that becomes the new mandate, then managers may find themselves participating in their own demise on the one hand and forced to contemplate a metamorphosis of their own on the other.

To suggest the full force of the analogy to business in general and to HR in particular, the educational trend would be comparable to employees being trained in various degrees to become employee managers while still remaining workers. How that might happen, what benefits it could provide, and finally what happens to principals in education and managers in business in the process first requires examining the education model.

Why and how did such replacement occur? What are the key change drivers? Although there are many, five points in particular are critical and bear a close parallel with HR trends and patterns.

1. *Empowerment.* Empowerment did not suddenly surface but was part of the long-term and gradual general empowering of employees. It was preceded by teachers initially serving on committees, then on site management councils, and finally on partnership teams of principals and teachers (Elmore 1996). That evolutionary process proceeded in stages: from receiving and sharing information, to making recommendations, and finally to making decisions.

2. *The impact of supervisors, good and bad.* The good ones encouraged greater participation by grouping employees into teams and then coaching team leaders on group dynamics and negotiation. Oppressive supervisors left no room for dissent, which they always treated as insubordination in any case. The resentment against such "bosses" led, when the occasion presented itself, to more assertive behaviors on the part of employees. Either way, teachers were gradually led or bullied into accepting wider responsibility and roles.

3. *Overload prevailed.* The plate was too full for school principals. Expected to do more, and more with less, they typically averaged 10–14 hour days, attended evening events, and took home paperwork over the weekend. In addition, their roles had been expanded to include public relations, legal counseling, acting as a social worker, community service, fund raising, and so forth. Something had to give, or take up the slack—sharing management came to the rescue.

4. *Shortages were looming.* The demographics of the baby boom generation was driving the need for substantial replacement. Recent employee projections suggest a major crunch in middle-level managers. The U.S. Department of Labor estimated that between 5,000 and 10,000 new principals would have to be hired by 2005. In addition, more will expect to be paid more, and proportionately more may be bilingual.

5. *Economics entered the picture in both internal and external forms.* Internally, managers and principals collectively were a significant cost item. The additional costs of the "office" of manager (personnel, equipment, phones, etc.) had to be factored in. Finally, the impact externally on quality products and services represents a serious and in many cases an unacceptable cost.

Given the above combination of push and pull, of challenge and response, of despair and incentives, it is perhaps less surprising that in education at least we now have schools operating without principals, with learning managers in charge. Teachers run the schools but maintain their direct involvement by remaining in the classroom (e.g., Ed/Visions in Minnesota). As a result there is closer integration and interfacing of administration and instruction than ever before. Outsourcing has become an intelligent and cost-saving norm. Cost control is firmly in place. Morale is high.

Students similarly have been involved in decision making. For example, in one school students sought to upgrade computers and software. There was no money in the budget. They were told to huddle and problem solve. They came back with the proposal that students would perform all the custodial duties currently outsourced to a cleaning service; the money saved would purchase the upgrades. And it has worked, and the quality of maintenance has remained high. The only downside was that when their parents learned of the arrangement, they demanded equal time at home.

But what was the nature of the teacher's leader training? More important for the focus here, who did it? It was the principals who alone had the education and the experience to design and to offer the workshops. In addition, they served as coaches to mentor induction and in the process also functioned as internal consultants. In other words, managers shifted their role from management to HR. Moreover, HR, which because of downsizing and outsourcing generally had been decimated, welcomed the addition of new competence and expertise. Finally, because managers regularly combine learning and leading, they were in the pivotal position of protecting and optimizing human capital and playing the role of learning officers. In short, principals discovered new roles and acquired new value. They experienced a parallel metamorphosis with those they were training. Far from participating in their own demise, they found new directions for the expression of their competence.

Can this model be applied to business with equally beneficial results? Probably, but only if it is gradually staged, and only if middle-level managers acting as HR practitioners are put in charge, become advocates of the process with senior staff, and undertake the necessary training. Part of that advocacy is requesting what most firms generally are unwilling to share: sub-budgets for individual units that are part of a division. Divisional budgets are common but not disaggregated beyond that level, but budget access and management is an absolute minimal empowering tool for transforming workers into managers. In fact, managing money turns out to be as important as managing people (Handy 1989).

The managerial agenda designed to develop the potentiality of employees as managers will require three basic stages: planning, implementing, and monitoring.

1. *Planning.* The value of putting managers in charge is that they understand that it is not so much the training as the implementation of the training that is important. They thus insist on not one but three planning tasks: planning the training, planning the implementation, and monitoring both. In other words, a totally integrated, hopefully seamless process. The training agenda should be collaboratively developed by a team of managers (Ratcliffe 2002). Role-playing of employees by HR and other supervisors would provide a test run and opportunity for correctives or additions. Finally, the agenda for training has to be designed in such a way that it can be phased and folded into the employee evaluation process. Building the upgrading process and goals into the employee evaluation process not only reinforces the training but also introduces the new and upgraded criteria for upgraded employee performance (Buchen 2003).

2. *Implementing.* Minimums, maximums, and optimums have to be identified in advance as the progressive goals of implementation. The suggested calendar is nine months to a year. The respective intervals for each stage are three or four months. End points and timetables have to be joined. In short, managers are expert at steering change, setting up stretch goals, and enforcing nonnegotiable timetables.

3. *Monitoring.* The group monitoring the program has to reflect the typical core competencies of managers. It has to range from finances to quality control, from worker morale to customer satisfaction, from prioritizing unit goals to aligning them with company objectives. No one else but managers can be that multitasked and

360-degrees focused except perhaps consultants. Even here they push the envelope further. As internal consultants, managers offer the best of both worlds. Finally, monitoring again taps special managerial knowledge; evaluations at prescribed intervals are offered in the form of balanced scorecards.

Will these options for business managers be embraced? Some would resist and refuse to cooperate in their own suicide. They would rather leave and relocate to other locations (and even countries) that still need good, old-fashioned, prodding, and directive managers. Evolution is uneven and at any given moment in time all stages coexist. But others may not like what is happening but grudgingly understand that intense competition has led to a double action: the need to increase employee productivity on the one hand and the need to reduce personnel costs on the other. With almost terrible inevitability, the two come together with the notion of employee managers. Like money, evolution is impersonal. It bears no malice or motive, and just asserts the inexorable law of change. And the next stage of evolution requires transferring the authority from managers to workers.

But far from signaling the end of management, if the options offered principals are any guide, managers may choose a different but no less challenging future. In fact, one can even argue that the management metamorphosis may place managers in the driver's seat of the learning organization (Van der Heijden 1996). By providing the future knowledge base as training designers and internal consultants, they may find a niche as valued as what they enjoyed before. If, as seems likely, companies are increasingly looking for chief learning officers, HR-driven managers would not only be a key source for such appointments but also manage the emergence of a new partnership: the fusion of learning and leadership.

REFERENCES

Argyris, C., and D. Schön. 1974. *Theory in practice: Increasing professional effectiveness*. San Francisco: Jossey-Bass.

Buchen, I. 2003. Employee mission statements. *PI* 40, no. 4.

————. 2000. Team management. *National Productivity Review* 24, no. 3.

Champy, James. 1999. *Reengineering management.* New York: HarperCollins.

Elmore, Richard. 1996. *Restructuring in the classroom: Teaching, learning, and school organization.* San Francisco: Jossey-Bass.

Greenleaf, Robert K. 1977. *Servant leadership.* Mahwah, N.J.: Paulist Press.

Hamel, C., and C. K. Prahalad. 1994. *Competing for the future.* Boston, Mass.: Harvard Business School Press.

Hammer, Michael, and James Champy. 1993. *Reengineering the corporation: A manifesto for business revolution.* New York: HarperCollins.

Handy, C. 1989. *The age of unreason.* Boston, Mass.: Harvard Business School Press.

Lambert, Linda. 2003. *Leadership capacity for lasting school improvement.* Alexandria, Va.: Association for School Curriculum and Design.

Ratcliffe, J. 2002. Scenario planning. *Foresight* 4, no. 1.

Ringland, Gill. 1998. *Scenario planning: Managing for the future.* Chichester, U.K.: Wiley.

Silverman, D. 1997. *Qualitative research.* London: Sage.

Van der Heijden, K. 1996. *Scenarios: The art of strategic conversations.* London: Wiley.

13

TESTING-EMBEDDED TRAINING: PREDICTIVE METRICS

Virtually all current discussion of training appears to be increasingly driven by return on investment. There is an incessant clarion call for designing complex digital dashboards, developing learning analytics, and installing follow-up data-tracking systems. Training has to justify itself. Human capital has to equal financial value. Learning management systems (LMS) have to be a profit center.

Who can argue with such accountability, especially when it is self-imposed or self-inflicted? But perhaps we have been too hasty to blur our difference from other functions, and too indiscriminate to recognize that we may be throwing out the baby with the dirty bath water. Already measurement has become our master and in the process eclipsed training content, just as in public education assessment has trumped curriculum development. Information technology is now enlisted as the infallible agent of performance documentation. Hopefully, training will emerge exonerated—but in the process, this poses at least three problems.

First, an old one: we measure only what is measurable. Thus, the intangibles that elude our yardsticks are either ignored or minimized. It is not unlike the high school principal who recently eliminated all museum trips because museums were not on the state tests. Or the English teacher in Chicago who was ordered to stop teaching Shakespeare because the bard has been dropped from the reading comprehension profile.

The second problem is more familiar and sinister, although it builds on the first. We teach to the test. Generally, meeting business objectives dictates content. Specifically, it determines what applications are taught. That way, measurement can offer a mirror match of success. The happy end justifies the means. The illustrative applications built into the training ensure a solid and positive fit.

But follow-up has revealed a disturbing applications gap. When new challenges required applications that went beyond the original illustrative sets, square pegs were being ground into round holes. This discrepancy was echoed recently when a group of expert math teachers surveyed the performance of outstanding math students and found the same lack of transference. Their explanation? Knowledge is not understanding. When assessment is limited to the range of applications introduced, the reading may be a false positive. Measurement should measure adaptability, not duplication.

Finally, testing generally occurs before and after training. It increasingly involves employee testing so that training can be diagnostically driven. Already noted is the current extensive preoccupation with follow-up. What is missing perhaps is a middle ground where measurement perhaps can be introduced directly into and concurrent with training. Aside from restoring instructional design to centrality, it may serve also to mitigate the other two problems noted above.

But to do so in turn rests on a key assumption: training as an environment. It embodies company culture. As such, it models the way the company at its best thinks, operates, and relates. As an agent of instruction, the training environment may also be used to introduce new elements such as the fusion of testing and training to shape and give new direction to that culture.

To embed testing in training requires a revision of instructional design. Both knowledge acquisition and cognitive learning must be blended and interactively assessed. In the process, the learner may have to become an increasingly active assessment partner. The goal of all training is not just knowledge but understanding. That alone ensures optimum adaptability and application. It also offers that rare assessment presumption—prediction.

Although training generally does not grade learners, all good instructors informally and unofficially assess not only their students' performance but also their future careers. When face-to-face training was the norm and when many trainers were also consultants or associated with HR, it was standard practice during lunch or dinner to compare notes. It was invariably predictive. Each one took turns identifying the high flyers and future stars. The consensus was remarkable.

In other words, the goal of testing during training ups the ante. Its sights are predictive. It is to anticipate not only the extent but also the flexibility of meeting company objectives and workplace stretch goals. It is both quantitative and qualitative, environmental and individual. But the development of predictive metrics is not an add-on or an overlay. It requires a total review of the dynamics of instructional design along the following lines:

1. Generic training has to be customized.
2. It must minimally minister to work and learner specifics.
3. Assessment of performance during training should be benchmarked against assessment of performance after training.
4. Ideally, all training assessments should be predictive.
5. The assessment process should be made an integral part of instructional design.
6. Measurement of knowledge acquisition and performance projections should be through learner self-assessment.
7. Predictive assessments are self-fulfilling prophecies.
8. In effect, learners increasingly teach, coach, and assess themselves.
9. Work and learner customizing of generic instruction is a learner-driven and learning task.
10. Data tracking should not be one-size-fits-all but adjusted to the degree and extent of learner involvement in assessment.

The key to predictive metrics is employee acceptance of a greater and more active role in their own development. Minimally, three shifts are involved. First, this should not be perceived as a break in the increasing use of employee testing but an expansion of its range now to include assessment ability. Second, it no longer limits judgment to end-of-course evaluations, but makes employees co-present with and coproducers of testing-embedded instruction from the outset. The result is not a separation but a fusion of assessment and instruction. Third, it links the role and level of learner involvement to the extent and level of data collection. Employees become data partners. Measurement is quantitative and qualitative, generic and customized. The relationship between these two assessment sources is a variable as noted below:

Level of Learner Involvement	Degree of Assessment
None	Total Data Tracking
Minimal	Data Tracking Plus Limited Self-Assessment
Maximum	Self-Coaching Customizing of Work and Learner
Optimum	Predictive Assessments of Autonomous Learner

Predictive metrics are being urged as the next stage of state-of-the-art instruction because they tap into three powerful related trends. The first is the recognition that maintaining and increasing productivity is a product of training. Only savvy and smart employees ensure gains. The learning curve establishes the profit curve. The second trend is knowledge and experience sharing. Whether those trained constitute an actual team, all instruction must crossover and become team knowledge. Chat rooms serve to share both individual and divisional information, experience, and expectations and to miniaturize company-wide commonality and diversity. The big picture, like big brother, is omnipresent. Third, customizing of training can only be accomplished by the greater employee participation of employees in both the learning process and its assessment. Testing-embedded training is but the newest step in an employee development curve that runs from learner dependence to learner autonomy. Predictive metrics are thus employee driven. In the process, self-fulfilling prophecies are not discouraged but welcomed and accommodated. The supreme goal is to preside over the shift from employees who not only work smarter but also are smarter managers of their work. Training has to raise the do-it-yourself process to the higher level of self-managing, self-organizing, and self-assessing employee managers. In short, the focus of training should be to help create and shape the future workforce.

14

WORK COVENANTS AS PROGRESSIVE EMPOWERMENT

Peter Block, author of *The Empowered Manager* (1987), in a recent article in *Executive Excellence* (May 2000) bluntly states: "Poorly managed and poorly led companies deserve to die." But what about the innocent? Why should the workers pay for the ineptitude of their leaders? Perhaps the standard for wars should be not how many soldiers but how many generals are killed.

Increasingly, employees are questioning those in charge and wondering how smart and anticipatory they really are. The first thing a savvy consultant does when brought in to solve a problem is talk to and listen to employees. Invariably, they not only know what is wrong but also how to fix it. But they are never asked.

Increasingly, employees are neither blinded by hero worship nor codependent on a father who knows best. They value their own intelligence and refuse to accept suffering the consequences of the incompetent and the paternalistic. Too many have endured the downsizings and reductions in force associated with mergers and acquisitions to have much confidence in a leadership that gives lip service to participation but essentially practices benevolent authoritarianism.

On the other side of the aisle a similar rebellion is brewing, only in this instance it involves managers. Thinning or flattening out the organization has made overwork a norm. Fewer managers are being asked to accomplish and supervise more, to fill in gaps left by loss, and to rely on less-qualified workers to accomplish ambitious "stretch" goals. Moreover, to do all that, they have to create, train, and sustain worker teams. Afterward, they have little or nothing to manage. The team does it all. As managers become aware that they are being asked to cut their own throats, they are less than enthusiastic about supporting teams whose increasing effectiveness increases productivity but forecasts their own demise. In short, there is discontent on both sides.

Workers want more say; managers seek to preserve their status. Employees want to become not just shareholders but stakeholders. Managers want their expertise of planning and supervision valued. Workers argue that their experience is critical, managers their education and training. The net result is an impasse. Employees will not surrender their recently achieved centrality, nor will managers—after all the years of dominance—quietly take a back seat. But, alas, the rope in this tug of war is the organization that employs both. When the CEOs or senior staff speak on behalf of the organization, all the familiar declarations come from the mount: we are in charge, we set policy and choose direction, we determine who is hired and who is fired—in short, we rule.

Not so any more. Too many major misjudgments, flawed products or services, failed companies, and unprofitability have torn or tarnished the mantle of infallibility. Moreover, the dissension on both sides of the aisle is generally ignored, and thus nothing or little is done to bridge or converge the two. Current CEOs and their senior staff preside over a divided house that is immune to traditional monarchial harmony and capacity to resolve.

The net result is wobbly three-legged stool. The CEOs and senior staff (and board of trustees) no longer provide constant support for managers because of the pressure for worker productivity. The managers in turn still have to do all the dirty work, fill in holes brought about by reductions in force, and trade off their traditional control with worker teams. The employees are becoming increasingly distrustful of upper management's judgment and resentful of their obscene salaries, often increased precisely when layoffs occur in some kind of perverse reward system.

In many organizations distrust has become the norm. Replacing CEOs solves credibility temporarily. But it is recognized soon as an external public relations game of duplicity as managers and workers see that no internal changes follow in its wake. In short, disunity reigns among the three major components of an organization: upper management, middle management, and rank and file. When surviving global competition is factored in, what follows is a total preoccupation with the bottom line. Then virtually everything and everyone becomes expendable.

The dilemma is clear: how do we put Humpty Dumpty together in a new way? Can a different alliance between the three major constituencies be forged or negotiated? If so, what is the glue? There are some tentative and partial signs that a new understanding and even re-rapprochement is gradually surfacing. The standard official negotiations between workers and their organizations have been extended unofficially between workers and managers. Some CEOs are willing to limit executive power to bring about internal alignment. They are beginning to understand that their central task as leaders is not to glorify their role but to find and proclaim areas of commonality. Increasingly, middle-level mangers are warming to their new and different tasks of being team leaders and coaches of improved performance. Employees are increasingly aware of the need for a less adversarial and more cooperative attitude and of their own productivity and creativity offsetting the lower wages of global competition.

In other words, historically we appear to have reached a major branch point in which all sides are more open to changing their fundamental relationships with each other and of producing a whole that hopefully may even be more than a sum of its contending and divisive parts. There is a need then to explore and to define—no matter how tentative the different roles of all the major participants may be—in what I have called collaborative work covenants. Although what is offered here is not prescriptive, it is based on perceptible changes of practice on the one hand and major shifts in the literature of leadership and empowerment on the other. If such covenants are to take hold, however, there cannot be any take-backs in the hard-won battle of employee empowerment. New interfaces born of mutuality and commonality must be found to close current gaps. In the process, private enterprise may find itself moving more in the direction of socialism than capitalism.

How are covenants and collaboratives different from their earlier predecessors, the social contract and union contracts? The most obvious is that
the focus is not limited to workers. In fact, the major problem is not elim-
inating adversarial relationships, which may be sometimes of contributory
value, but getting all three parties to the table together to negotiate or
renegotiate their roles with respect to each other. That, in turn, requires
all to acknowledge that what is at stake is the company itself and its future.
Indeed, that is the first and most important area of commonality to be acknowledged. The company may be owned by stockholders, but its fate belongs to all those who are there equally at the table. Each one brings his
or her special expertise to bear, yet that expertise is not exclusively held.
It is available for input and overlap from all the others as well.

In addition, whatever form the negotiation shapes, it will never be final or emerge in as a singular, legalistic, elaborate formulation. Rather,
it will be a mosaic, a series of clusters, a compilation of agreements of
understanding. It will also be consciously incomplete. Negotiations can
go only so far and then they must cease. The endless and often trivial details of union contracts cannot become the substitute for basic operating
principles guiding new relationships. Moreover, room must be left for
fleshing the skeleton and accommodating the subsequent contributions
of all those who have to implement the accord.

Unlike union contracts, which like bibles spell out every chapter and
verse, and which require often as many to monitor as to implement, a
work covenants is intentionally incomplete. It is routinely discontinuous
and preserves gaps. It compels constant dialogue and negotiation on
every level and between every division and unit.

In addition, it is defined not so much in terms of the individual but
the group or team. And there are no jurisdictional limits; nothing is out
of bounds. If the team lacks anything, it can be imported. The group
may have a core, but its periphery and final extent may vary with the focus and the process. It is free to expand and even cross divisional boundaries in pursuit of its quarry. And when that happens successfully, new
configurations of operations may emerge, not even anticipated in the
original agreements Structural dexterity follows goal pursuit. Form
catches up and supports function.

But no addendum to the contract is required to freeze this new variation. To etch spontaneous change in stone and finalize its shape may

preclude a different configuration from emerging at another time and for another purpose. If anything, the work covenant process resembles the metaphor of a river flowing through an organization described and extolled by Margaret Wheatley (Wheatley and Kellner-Rogers 1996). Self-learning and self-organizing, the process affects the fundamental structure and culture of the company and brings about changes gradually from within. The organizational chart itself no longer imposes order from without but benchmarks change points. It is the history of a work constantly in progress.

Lest all this appear easy or rapid, it does not happen without extensive and intensive reconceptualization of work and work relationships by all the members of the triad. Effective groups attuned to process rather than function are not born. They have to be made, remade, nurtured, coached, and challenged. They are newly created. In other words, there is the need for all to master at least five group dynamics skills.

First, conflict is a norm. Managing opposition is the key to higher levels of understanding and performance. Second, interdependence of teams becomes the model for all. If a worker is dependent or codependent, he must become more independent. But ultimately workers and all others have to become more interdependent, not at the expense of their individuality but in addition to it. They have to become a new composite: collectivized individuals. Third, transition has to be accepted as a dominant and recurrent norm. Paradoxically, it provides the overriding and ambiguous benefit of an organization permanently in flux and committed to the dynamic give and take of collaboration. Fourth, work covenants require constant negotiation and persuasion. The process is endlessly consultative. The agreements reached are always tentative and situational. How they are arrived at is as important as what is finally agreed upon. It is an optimizing skill. Fifth and finally, communication must be constant and total. It is the stuff of mutual empowerment and a way of leaving no one behind or outside the circle. Persuasion is the key to bringing groups back together into new wholes, healing wounds in the process, and forging a new consensus. Again and again the recurrent summary and debriefing has to include the same litany: "OK. What have we learned? Where have we been? Where are we now? What is our future focus?"

The skills must be supplemented by an understanding and examination of the assumptions, expectations, and agenda of each group. Often

that requires reflection, assumptions analysis, and subsequent unlearning. For example, CEOs believe they have a monopoly on leadership.
Managers are convinced that workers must be managed. Workers often
think they know more than their immediate supervisors or the top brass.
But a central covenant value is the self-organizing principle of groups
managing themselves.

Overcoming limits to productivity may require that the traditional
distinctions between workers and managers be blurred. Workers assume managerial roles and managers assume worker roles. This is the
ultimate cross-training. It is also the key to how and why covenants can
also accommodate managers. Managerial functions are thus shared and
are not the monopoly of one class of employees. But aside from the
commonality of training and objectives that now tie both groups together, what is also required is a different definition of leadership.

It is not enough to claim that leadership is shared. Expertise is leadership, and it must be acknowledged and given its due at all levels of di-
rectives, or initiatives will not be hearkened to or respected. Such recognition means that every level leads. Each one not only possesses and
practices its unique version of stewardship but also is responsible for
harmonizing all the others as well.

Traditionally, shaping the whole was the distinction or cross that top
management alone had to bear. Bits and pieces of the cross were
parceled out to managers so that they could serve as mini-leaders. That
pecking order pecked at and muzzled or minimized the leadership of
each level below CEO. But the work covenant functions not unlike the
way a multidisciplinary task force does: the whole belongs to the whole.
It not only grants all a common purpose and focus but also the collective responsibility for sustaining and, if necessary, altering it. The
covenant thus defines and celebrates commonality.

One of the key problems of effective group collaboration is keeping
in front of everyone the big picture and not passing off a half as a whole.
Indeed, the primary responsibility of all leaders at all levels is to preserve and optimize the collective individuality of the group so that the
full force of its diversity can be brought to bear on all problems and opportunities. Finally, one of the key distinctions of such groups is in fact
the creation of the collectivized individual who epitomizes the behavioral and cultural power of work covenant collaboration.

What might a work collaborative look like? And how would it work? Perhaps a defining way of rendering that is to offer a profile of each of the four members of the trinity after the negotiation. It should be noted that they have not been blurred into each other. Each set of characteristics has been developed to focus on what is now within their altered power and province and how they now contribute to the process of creating new interfaces and a new set of working relationships.

THE ROLE OF TOP MANAGEMENT

The role of top management is to:

- Constantly draw, shape, and share the big picture, routinely, periodically.
- Not summarily announce or promulgate decisions; instead, provide persuasive reasons and documentation for decisions.
- Align policies with vision and mission and be value driven.
- Be proactive, anticipatory, future-driven.
- Conceive and present initiatives in clusters of alternatives and tradeoffs.
- Recognize, reward, and value innovation, small or large.
- Be intellectually rigorous, savvy, interesting, and occasionally daring.
- Signal clearly that the era of top-down, heavy-handed punitive bossism is dead and buried.
- Give to get: if you want more accountability, offer more choice.
- Finally, always tell the truth, especially if it is bad news.

MIDDLE-LEVEL MANAGERS

The role of middle-level managers is to:

- Minimize no's; maximize yes's; optimize maybe's.
- Not play the blame, shame, or gotcha game; go for root cause.
- Not play favorites.
- Be a straight shooter and talker.

- Be a worker; get your hands dirty.
- Not oppose or suppress opposition; incorporate it.
- Keep the customer alive and in everyone's face, every time and everywhere.
- Listen always; especially two-eared listening—hear what is said and what is not.
- Develop everyone you touch. Recognize that success is always multiple.

WORKERS

The role of workers is to:

- Have a say and stake in everything.
- Not allow yourself to be treated like a child and accept pablum when you have the teeth to chomp steak.
- Claim that expertise resides with workers.
- Remember that no one knows the job better than the one who does it.
- Constantly ask, discuss, and explore.
- Act as if there are no limits to individual and group development and capacity.
- Acknowledge that all are collectively responsible for what is done, said, and sold.
- Treat everyone with respect and dignity.
- Value the diversity of commonality and commonality of diversity: everybody is the same in a different way.
- Practice what is preached.

TEAMS EXHIBITING THE COLLABORATIVE WORK COVENANT

Together, you can:

- Create a team that is change ready, able to shift direction and focus as needed.

- Be intolerant of mediocrity in everything: quality of product, service, communication.
- Shape the values of the collaborative work covenant to align with the vision of the company and vice versa.
- Be smart about your industry; position your company to take advantage of emerging trends.
- Minimize bureaucracy—weeds push out flowers.
- Be obsessive about customers.
- Meet them, talk to them.
- Recognize that the customer is data. He may not be always right, but that is still the challenge.
- Move authority closest to the point of action and expertise.
- Examine stats.
- Challenge assumptions.
- Check alignments vertically, and to the right and left.
- Give a prize for the best question of the week.
- Create employee universities in which teams teach.
- Create happiness, camaraderie, and enthusiasm as a unique expression of the team, but never use it to shut out newcomers.
- Always seek to be interesting.
- Recognize and embody Blanchard's dictum: "None of us is as smart as all of us."

In many ways, collaborative worker covenants are being built upon previous breakthroughs and hard-won achievements. But these new agreements in many other ways are basically new. They signal a new competing centrality. No longer is the spotlight solely or even largely on CEOs, managers, or employees. Rather, the focus is on the interfacing relationships between them. Commonality is king. Just as the commons of the old village is what is shared and owned ay all, all collectively shape a new organizational configuration. Both vertical and horizontal alignments can be retained but only if surrounded and enclosed by a series of multiple concentric circles of common cause and purpose. The circular thus governs the architecture because all the knights of the Round Table are equal and all are leaders. Jurisdictional boundaries are no longer sacred. Everything must flow and meander like Wheatley's river through the entire enterprise.

Leadership is not the monopoly of the CEO or senior management. Leadership is distributed and written into everyone's job description. Cross-training and work interchangeability are common best practices. Above all, collaborative work covenants hopefully create a new and interesting home for a new kind of worker-manager-leader as a collectivized individual.

To many, perhaps, the prospect of such a covenant appears utopian. But given the realities of the economics of competition on the one hand and the forces of empowerment and commonality on the other, workplace collaboratives and covenants may emerge merely as the embodiment of a transitional present and a transitional future.

How do things change? Three ways: we will it, we negotiate it, and it just happens. Those who claim to be in charge of making and shaping change, whatever their level and fulcrum, would have us believe that the last member of the trinity is also within their province. It has no separate power or even identity except what they give to it. On a national and international level, the counterclaims of history—past, present, and emerging—are not allowed to prevail over forged policy and image. But the truth is otherwise. Andre Gide correctly noted that "we believe we possess when in reality we are possessed."

We should will and shape with vision and mission. We should seek to become masters of our fate. We also should sometimes achieve those ends by the less dramatic and self-glorifying means of tweaking, revising, recasting—all the ways we serve and honor adjusting to our times, challenges, and circumstances. But we must also develop a healthier respect for and tolerance of the extent to which we are determined from without, no matter what that does to our self-definition and esteem.

History in partnership with emerging trends is the DNA of change. Circumstances drive decisions. If the illusion of control is still important, then we designate transformation as a paradigm shift. We may be impacted from without, but at least it takes place with the permission of our conscious understanding.

The argument here is cumulative. Over the last two decades what has gradually, increasingly, and tenaciously determined change and the responses to it is enfranchisement—especially of the bottom at the expense of the middle and the top. In scope and intensity, it is comparable to the exodus from Egypt and the writing of the Declaration of Independence.

Neither event resulted in immediate and total freedom, which not only evolved but also was shaped, negotiated, and enshrined in vision and mission. Thus, willful self-determination still plays a critical role, but it is not self-initiating. At worst it is reluctant; at best, responsive. But willy-nilly, history holds the trump card.

To appreciate how pervasive and invasive empowerment has been, one needs to review the matrix below, which features in various categories what was in place before empowerment (BE) and after empowerment (AE).

No commentary is necessary. The visual display says it all.

EMPOWERMENT MATRIX

Categories	BE	AE
1. Structure	Centralized	Decentralized
	Vertical	Horizontal
2. Job Description	Prescribed	Self-Directed
3. Mission Statement	Organizational	Employee
4. Operations	Function	Process
5. Employees	Workers	Assets
6. Leadership	Specified	Distributed
	Top Down	Available
7. Pay	Salary	Gains-Sharing
8. Human Resources	Recruitment	Retention
9. Relationships	Individual	Group
	(Independence)	(Interdependence)
10. Training	Homogeneous	Heterogeneous
	Singular	Cross-Divisional
11. Information	Hoarded	Shared
12. Performance	Blame/Shame	Improvement
13. Manager	Boss	Coach
14. Listening	Limited/Selective	Feedback/Feedforward
15. Decisions	Top Down	Consensual
16. Innovation	R&D	Learning Organization
17. Forecasting	Planners	Lay Forecasting
18. Agreements	Contracts	Covenants
19. Voice	Singular	Multiple
20. Roles	Given	Negotiated

REFERENCES

Block, Peter. 2000. Accountability for results. *Executive Excellence* (May).

———. 1987. *The empowered manager: Positive political skills at work.* San Francisco: Jossey-Bass.

———. 1993. *Stewardship.* San Francisco: Berrett-Koehler.

Wheatley, Margaret, and Myron Kellner-Rogers. 1996. Self-organization, strategy and leadership. *Strategy and Leadership* (Strategic Leadership Forum) 24 (July–August): 18–24.

15

LEARNING THEORY-THERAPY CROSSOVER: A FUTURE TRAINING DIRECTION?

With the increasing use of employee testing and the development of predictive metrics, is there a danger of invasion of privacy? Might we be crossing over into forbidden personal areas? It is a genuine dilemma hastened by the linkages of learning theory with learning therapy. But perhaps there is middle way that involves the internal and external dynamics of being both self-centered and interpersonal at the same time. In one comprehensive and integrated arc, learning therapy houses who we are, how we have come to be that way, our values, how we relate, how we learn, how we work, and how we work together. Combining cognition and psychology, learning therapy encompasses not only how we can learn but also how we learn with and from others, and ultimately how we can change, repair, and extend knowing relationships. Hence, the emergence of learning as therapy and therapy as learning.

This is important for a number of reasons:

1. Learning therapy (LT) provides training with a wider, more inclusive starting point.
2. LT creates a new relationship framework as an instructional design focus.
3. Both the range and depth of instructional design can be extended to explicitly link workers to each other.

4. LT also can lead to a more self-critical awareness of work as mutual dependency.
5. Work can be redefined not solely as job parts but as a series of job relationships.
6. Interpersonal relationships and skills themselves can be perceived as both a learning and therapy experience.
7. The privacy issue is less of an issue because learning therapy provides both neutral and neural paths that are more generalized, objective, and justifiably accessible.
8. LT training may have a better chance of taking hold by having an internalized base.
9. The typical workshop on getting along with difficult people, for example, may ultimately involve fusing the psychology of being difficult with the cognition of being resistant to change.
10. The entire training menu may benefit from being reviewed by and expanded with the powerful supplement of learning therapy.

If such a review, following up that last item, were undertaken, and learning therapy were applied to communication and leadership, what might be some of the yields of applying learning therapy?

1. Basic workshops on communications skills or leadership development can be enhanced by an overlay of learning relationships.
2. Clarity of expression and power positions would be reconceived as interpersonal relationships.
3. The motives and modes of communication may be determined not only by attitudes toward the subject matter but also by the personalities at the giving and receiving ends.
4. Similarly, effective leadership may be shown to rest not only on decision-making skills but also on the capacity for empathy.
5. Effective communication and leadership ultimately can be perceived not just as skills or knowledge but also as ways to learn and to heal.
6. Wired in place, this newly fused approach closes gaps, enriches relationships, and above all establishes commonality and shared understanding.
7. It thus can help to create a genuine learning community that works and learns together.

But how to make it happen? What are the essentials of learning therapy? What are its dynamics? Happily, it is a building-block process. Five major stages are involved. They are not separate but progressive, not exclusive but inclusive, not sequential but cumulative. Together, they simulate a total learning therapy journey.

LEARNING THERAPY PRIMER 101

1. Compiling a personal inventory
2. Identifying its operating values
3. Portraying its operating relationships
4. Assessing the learning potential of that inventory
5. Linking the personal inventory and learning potential to job performance

Throughout, learning therapy always focuses on three major relationship clusters: self, others, and teams. Thus, each of the five steps would be always rendered multiple times, as shown in table 15.1.

Each item above also can be given aspirational and futures-directed dimensions, as follows:

Current	Future
1. This is who I am.	This is who I want to be.
2. This is what I value.	This is what I want to value more.
3. This is how I relate.	This is how I wish to relate differently.
4. This is how I learn.	This is how I unlearn and change.
5. This is how I work.	This is how I work more productively.

The final assignment of Learning Therapy 101 is for each participant to assemble a composite profile using selectively the input from the above five areas. Here is a sample:

My name is Sally B. I work in assembly section B. I have always had a strong sense of who I am and my worth. My folks gave me that. So family is probably what is most important to me. I find it hard to understand those who don't believe in a strong family. I trust my bosses or supervisors.

Table 15.1 Learning Therapy's Three Major Relationship Clusters

1. Personal Inventory and Profile—"This is who I am."

Subject	Lines of Inquiry	Influences	Goals
a. Self	Who am I?	Familial impact?	What satisfies me?
b. Others	How do I relate?	Where did I learn that?	How can I change?
c. Team	Responses to authority	Friendships?	Sharing and trusting?

2. Values Profile—"This is what is important to me."

Subject	Beliefs	Moral Mentors	Behaviors
a. Self	Family? Achievement?	Memorable	Right and wrong
b. Others	Equal treatment	Values	Open-minded
c. Team	Diversity	Team Leaders	Respect

3. Relationships—"This is how I relate."

Subject	Family	Friends	Coworkers
a. Self	Keep intact	Like family	Civility
b. Others	Their commitment	Acquaintances	If possible, buddies
c. Team	Another family	Trust	Satisfaction

4. Assessing Learning Potential over Time—"This is how I learn."

Time Focus	Learning Successes/Blocks	What Works/What Doesn't
a. Child/Teen/Adult	Recollections list	In previous workshops
b. Others	With certain teachers	With certain supervisors
c. Teams	Sports plus other teams	Team knowledge level

5. Linkage of Inventory and Learning to Job Performance—"This is how I work."

Focus	Work Values	Job Performance	Job Learning/Growth
a. Self	What's important?	Evaluations	Gains/losses
b. Others	Working together	Interpersonal ratings	Team learning
c. Team	Innovation	Collective achievements	Group stretch

I guess they are sort of father figures to me. I prefer their giving us directions or telling us what to do rather than all this discussion about options. The supervisor knows more than all of us put together anyhow. Besides, he has his marching orders.

I usually get along with others. I am a hard worker; so I like to work with hard workers. I have a hard time with goof-offs. I cut people a lot of slack, give them enough rope to hang themselves. When they do, that's it. I will be civil but that's as far as I will go. If you are lucky enough to be a member of good, tight team, that is heaven. You could not ask for anything better than that. They become a family of friends. Sometimes they are so good they lead themselves.

I never was good in school. I just graduated high school by the skin of my teeth. So I was kind of surprised that in some of the training I learned a lot. What's more, I put it to good use on the job. In one class which I loved, the instructor took me aside and praised me for my participation. I was embarrassed. I told him I always thought I was so dumb in high school, and here I am taking to it like a duck to water. He told me that I am at a different place now in my development; and high school might have been too far away from work to engage my interest and intelligence. I could feel my cheeks flush when he praised my intelligence. What a wonderful thing to say to me! He reminded me of Father Ryan, who was like a second dad to me.

Working in a terrific team and learning how to be more productive and innovative has resulted in the best evaluations I have ever had. Going through this five-step exercise also has taught me a lot about myself, my job, and my relationships. I find that I am now into everything I do. Work has become personal. It might as well be that way because of all the time I spend here. It also helped me a write a better self-evaluation. But what I liked best about it all is how it changed my attitude toward the future and where I can be. Or as we always say in the team: This is Operation Leap Frog—while we are catching up, let us also get ahead.

With the approach of learning therapy, training can be grounded in employee identity and centrality. Moreover, it is noninvasive and it does not pry. It is a voluntary exercise of self-study and self-review. In the process, it establishes explicit and key links between employee and work, between personal values and work behaviors and relationships, and between individual learning styles and performance improvement. It situates all learning in behaviors and thus identifies the key motivators for and goals of change. Above all, it compels employees to perceive relationships as a key source of knowledge. Such relationships, when strong and mutual, also provide employee satisfaction—and thereby suggest that getting and giving satisfaction are contributions of all employees. Finally, it urges altering and improving relationships as a key way of increasing learning and job performance.

Learning therapy offers a new vantage point from which to restart or reposition employee relationships and training. It can stir greater employee involvement in both personal and professional terms. Employees literally can significantly increase their investment and ownership of the company. Moreover, the currency they use is their own. Finally, learning therapy can stir future development. Linking and aligning such personal and professional growth with that of the company more than pays back any training investment in the therapy of learning.

II

FTLL, MULTIPLE INTELLIGENCES, AND LEARNING DIVERSITY

16

PROGRESSIVE AND CIRCULAR PROBLEM SOLVING

A classic formulation of the problem-solving process involves three stages: Know-What, Know-How, and Know-Why. The first involves tapping the knowledge of what one knows. The second brings to bear what one has learned from the applications of such knowledge. Finally, the third draws upon the systemic knowledge of how things and people interact to solve problems and to implement solutions.

That all sounds so sensible and logical. But at least three concerns surface:

1. *Sequence.* One can argue that the last should really be the first. Problem solving should be not only methodological but also thoughtful, data driven, and conceptual. It should be also an interactive thinking and learning experience. If Know-Why were first, learning would join thinking from the outset. The two would constantly task each other and in the process raise the level of both as well as the quality of the solution. In short, the questions asked and in what order determines whether the problem-solving process is progressive or circular (a single or double loop).

2. *Hidden drama of interplay.* Typically, the problem solver remains removed and apart from the problem. He (or she) is the subject

examining an object. But he does not question or examine how his methodological approach or even how his perception of the problem might contribute and alter the object. He would not hesitate calling for more data or information if needed, but hardly ever pauses to reflect on what he and his method unknowingly may bring to the process. Indeed, the need for Know-Why might not only be in the wrong order but also needs to be applied both to the problem and to the problem solver.

3. *Fit.* There is not one problem-solving system. A number of factors determine selection. Which one to tap often proceeds from the recognition that there are different orders of complexity as well as levels of expectations on both the problem and solution sides. Goals also determine choice. It makes an enormous difference whether the objective is improvement or innovation. Finally, the organizational culture plays a key role in favoring and shaping the preferred problem-solving mode (e.g., GE always and only uses Six Sigma).

Regardless of approach, what is clear is that problem solving is perhaps the most dominant and dominating activity of the entire workforce from top to bottom. Indeed, how one solves may be how one succeeds. According to Gardner, that it is also how cultures think, learn, and ultimately lead. In short, knowing where to place Know-Why determines whether the thinking, learning, and leading trinity is progressive or circular, whether it leads to greater understanding and adaptability, and finally whether it confers the ultimate gift of innovation. Happily, multiple intelligences (MI) multiplies and enriches both progressive and circular problem solving.

PROGRESSIVE PROCESS

Progressive problem solving is linear sequential; that is, it goes forward in a straight and tight series of incremental steps or gains. It is thus always additive. It is a series of statements, not questions. It reflects the use of a singular intelligence. It is always a checklist. Here is how it marshals data and information to move through its essential stages.

Know-What
1. Raw Data (unlabeled and without direction) (know-what)
2. Data Categorized (now designated and ordered)
3. Data Formatted (now is information)
Know-How
4. Information Applied (now knowledge)
Know-Why
5. Knowledge Applied (problem solved)

CIRCULAR AND MULTIPLE PROCESS

The circular does not abandon the linear sequential but encloses it. It also not only begins with Know-Why but uses that question as its constant spearhead and prod. Three specific areas are brought into play: data (Know-What), methodology, and end goals.

Thus, the first three steps above now are multiplied and become subject to five questions:

- What do we know?
- What don't we know?
- What don't we know we don't know?
- What is enough to know to problem solve?
- What can we learn that we did not know from the process?

Next methodology multiply perceived is folded into the inquiry process:

- What kind of thinking shapes our characteristic problem-solving mode?
- What assumptions do we bring to the problem that may require its being redefined or repositioned?
- What can be learned or discovered that can be built into the problem solving process?

Finally, end goals as drivers and assessment:

- Have we got it right, given the goals?
- Have we got it as right as we can get it?

- Have we simulated? Can it live, thrive, and function in real time, with real people, in a real world?
- Does the solution have a future?
- Does the problem have a greater future than the solution?

Of course, not all problems are complicated and need to be multiply approached. Many are straightforward and can be solved quickly and progressively. But the argument here is that much of what is new and discontinuous has left its mark on the emergence of new and disconcerting problems.

1. More and more of current problems are of a different, more contrary, and intractable nature. As such, they are not as amenable to the conventional fast progressive mode—although that may not stop its knee-jerk use.
2. Information technology tracking is now more dynamic. It exists in real time and just in time. It is more instructive and renders processes transparent and accessible while they are in motion. Analogy in the medical field is going from MRIs to fMRIs. The later records and measures brain activity in response to a variety of different kinds of questions asked. Such data flow and tracking now increasingly eludes the calipers of progressive problem solving.
3. The ante has been upped from continuous improvement to continuous innovation. Once a different future and innovation enter and drive the scheme of things, standard problem solving is not enough. What is needed is more—more multiple, more circular, more holistic thinking, learning, and leading. One creative source of such enrichment and amplification is multiple intelligences.

17

MULTIPLE INTELLIGENCES, COGNITIVE SCIENCE, AND GENETICS

It is important at the outset to identify the origin of multiple intelligences (MI) as both physiological and psychological. Its originator, Howard Gardner, came to gradually recognize its existence through the study of brain-damaged patients. From the beginning then, MI was thus experimentally linked to brain research and appears as a seminal version of later cognitive science.

In the process, his work involved challenging the singular measure of IQ and arguing for the norm of multiple talents displayed through discretely identifiable multiple intelligences. The three key texts that expound his essential arguments are *Frames of Mind* (1983), *The Unschooled Mind: How Children Think and How Schools Should Teach* (1991), and *Multiple Intelligences* (1993).

Howard Gardner first presented his concept of multiple intelligences in his book *Frames of Mind*—a significant title. He also explained how his work with brain-damaged children and adults contributed to his rejection of the singular intelligence of IQ and his advocacy for multiple forms of intelligence. He identified the criteria used to screen the categories of intelligence and linked each criteria and each intelligence to specific areas of the brain. He initially identified seven intelligences. Ten years later Gardner published his by-now definitive statement on

MI and in the process added an eighth intelligence: naturalist. (Two others have been suggested—existential and futuristic, which would round it out to ten intelligences.)

The special value of *The Unschooled Mind* (1991) is that Gardner here explicitly addresses how children think and how schools should teach (the subtitle of his book). The thinking process is dubbed the learning pathways of the mind. Thus, to Gardner, from the outset thinking and learning are permanently paired. Thinking-Learning always proceeds through four stages: data, information, knowledge, and understanding. Later, a fifth will be added—innovation. But the first and most pervasive puzzle or problem Gardner identifies is the failure of schools (and perhaps all institutions) to value and teach real understanding of subject matter.

He cites various studies that document how even high-scoring students in math, science, and the humanities fail to apply what they have learned beyond the problem sets presented as part of the original instruction. Gardner concludes that such a failure is one of confusing knowledge with understanding. To structure his discussion further along developmental lines, he then identifies three kinds of learners: intuitive (preschool), scholastic (K–12), and disciplinary (12–16). His focus on the first serves to establish the basic building blocks and leaning pathways.

Gardner reviews the various studies of the mind of the child. He cites Piaget and those who came after him. He examines and accepts the recent work of Chomsky and others who regard language as a reflection of both mental and cultural processes of the young child. In other words, Gardner seeks to bridge biology and culture, brain research and language development, as they shape the cognition of the infant.

THE WORLD OF THE PRESCHOOLER

Perhaps the most startling discovery is that the infant sensory apparatus and mind is in many ways the same as that of adults. Infants, for example, see color as spectrum and easily match colors groups, as do chimpanzees. The same is true of auditory and movement distinctions of infants. Above all, what becomes clear is that such discriminations are not learned but inborn, and support later learning.

In similar fashion, the infant is also pretuned to know other persons and the social world. The infant engages in lively mimetic exchanges and responses to adults and their facial and language cues. Finally, no matter how inborn and automatic the linkages of sensory and motor response are, they begin to acquire cultural configurations as the infant enters the social world; and these new acquisitions are learned or acquired, not inborn. The power of the original sensory touchstones, in fact, is so totally obscured by later knowledge that almost all suffer from "infantile amnesia"—well, not totally.

What emerges from the further development of the preschooler is a symbolic repertoire manifested particular in creative play: drawing, building blocks, modeling clay, and so on. The child develops symbolic scripts of play that he can communicate to and involve other children with, and even instruct adults mimetically in the rules of play. Gardner finally identifies a number of basic stages of development and increasing symbolic sophistication of the preschool child up to the age of six. These will serve as the foundations on which the school will build. But if the new knowledge of school is in conflict with the way the child has made sense of the world, the child may falter and fail.

In summary, then, the world of the infant and the preschooler is surprisingly rich, varied, and complex. But the most striking discovery is that the infant is programmed from birth genetically to be a learning machine. Learning is built into the way the infant is wired and driven by sensory impulses that are inbred. In other words, the period from infancy to age six constitutes the preschool of the child where children acquire knowledge, language, and socialization. Play is the way children learn. Sadly, often the first command they receive in school is that this is a place for work, not play.

Learning and School Goals and Measures

Gardner examines schools as key institutions with their own values and traditions and also from the point of view of the world of the preschooler. He claims that schools are designed according to the goals of the society. Three options are described. The first asks the school to prepare the young for later life, careers, and citizenry roles. The second identifies prized areas of knowledge to be acquired. The third—Gardner's choice—opts for understanding.

If understanding, not just knowledge, is the goal, a transformative approach is required. The teacher's role is to create or identify challenging situations or simulations that can be used to discover and unearth the knowledge that establishes the basis for understanding. But the way learning is assessed determines whether the goal of understanding prevails.

What the school and the community value is what they test. If what is being tested proves somewhat difficult, intractable, or "unamenable" to statistical tallies, then the material has to be reconfigured to minister to the test. In short, there is often a mismatch between the statistical agenda of the school and the basic inclinations of human learning. Teaching to the test is thus often doubly reductive and distortive.

Matching Learning Pathways and Subject Matter

Gardner examines the problems posed by teaching subject matter. In large part, these problems grew out of a number of historical changes, two in particular. In the 19th century, less than 10 percent of the school population attended secondary school. The rest were essentially provided only with the basic literacies of the three R's. But with the mandate at the beginning of the 20th century for universal education, schools had to offer the basic academic disciplines to all, uniformly taught and to the same extent, all across the country. In short, schools became a dominant educating and socializing institution.

Still, the key issue for Gardner is, Schooling for what end? Gardner's answer remains, Understanding. He notes that there are basically two ways of knowing, both embedded in infancy. One is the sensorimotor way of knowing as described by Piaget. The other is symbolic way of knowing that relies on interactive systems such as language and play relationships. If no schooling or learning interventions occur, the child will continue to develop but at a slower or more moderate pace. Problems occur when the various disciplines presented are in conflict with the child's basic way of knowing.

After detailing misconceptions in teaching physics, biology, math, humanities, arts, history, and literature, Gardner offers three concluding explanations for those misconceptions. First, many teachers themselves do not possess understanding of their subject matter. Second, the few that do fail to communicate it effectively. Third, the understanding taught is not properly assessed. If it were, its absence would be apparent.

THE SOLUTION OF A MULTIPLE ENVIRONMENT

He raises the issue of what would be a most promising environment for converting knowledge into understanding. Unexpectedly, he cites Project Spectrum, which is a school in a museum and which blends the strengths of each and requires young students to learn as apprentices.

To Gardner, no one flunks museum. It is also a place of daily discovery, where new notions are recorded and encouraged and where the range of subjects is a miniature of the whole. Above all, the joint school-museum provides the occasion for reintroducing Gardner's MI and multiple assessments. Gardner concedes that significant gains also can come about through other means and environments, such as whole language and early science programs.

Gardner then moves up to middle-school environments and projects that understandably make even greater use of MI and of assessment tools such as videotape and daily reporting to emphasize the importance of the communication process as demonstrating understanding. Often the audience is broadened to include community presentations as well as tapping the resources of the community. Finally, although technology now has increasingly entered the picture, the key ingredients to Gardner are multiple environments, intelligences, and assessments (especially reflective self-assessments).

Gardner values museums as learning environments and project learning because both sustain and optimize MI and multiple assessments. They also develop community links and place great emphasis on communication, emphasizing student participation in self-assessment through reflection. What is noteworthy is that there is little or no difference between elementary and middle school students and projects as long as they are set up at adjusted apprentice levels.

Gardner completes the cycle by paying special attention to high school students, although inevitably his views are cumulative and circular. Thus, he notes that there are three kinds of physics taught: gut physics, lay physics, and physicist physics, respectively elementary, middle, and high school. The basic problem is that the three kinds of physics are used to repudiate or belittle each other rather than to build on and connect with each other. The other mistake is to postpone or reserve the later complexities for older kids when the dynamics can begin to coexist side by side with the gut and lay stages.

Gardner goes on to describe other innovations in math, arts, and humanities for adolescents but pauses often to stress assessment. In particular he favors portfolios (or, as he calls them, "process-folios") because their function is to record the steps and stages, including missteps, of the learning process. In fact, he calls for the creation of the process-folio culture.

But he acknowledges that perhaps the most serious strategic problem that still remains is outmaneuvering singularity. The basic problem is one teacher, one textbook, one curriculum being offered a class of 25 different and diverse learners. Gardner's answer is to develop minimally five approaches, like five doors to the same room. Although less than the total number of eight intelligences, Gardner settles for the narrational, logical/quantitative, philosophical/foundational, aesthetic, and the existential. Finally, he claims that these five avenues can serve as a national and even global curriculum in support of teaching understanding.

SUMMARY

The two overriding themes of all of Gardner's work are multiplicity and understanding—multiple ways of knowing and assessing, and a deep and thorough understanding of disciplines. The reason he reaches for and seeks national and even global acceptance is that he is convinced that both themes not only are universal but also wired in place in every infant, cultural diversity notwithstanding.

The principal basic findings of multiple intelligences thus are:

- Intelligence is not singular but multiple.
- Such richness is there from birth.
- MI constitutes the universal learning pathways.

- All infants and preschoolers are programmed to be learning machines.
- Play is the earliest and remains the most enduring way to think, learn, and create.
- Adult play requires overcoming infant amnesia.
- Schools and learning fail when they ignore the basic thinking pathways of the brain.
- Understanding is the end and test of knowledge.
- Assessing understanding no matter how difficult the ultimate challenge.
- Thinking is the way we learn and learning is the way we think.

When these findings converge, we lead and are led. We thus are comfortable with paradox and being circular. We now can manage not only change but also ambiguity. And when such thinking, learning, and leading are at work in our institutions and businesses, the result is continuous improvement, intelligence, and innovation.

REFERENCES

Gardner, Howard. 1983. *Frames of mind: The theory of multiple intelligences.* New York: Basic Books.

———. 1991. *The unschooled mind: How children think and how schools should teach.* New York: Basic Books.

———. 1993. *Multiple intelligences: The theory in practice.* New York: Basic Books.

(18)

THE OPTIMAL TAXONOMY OF
HUMAN LEARNING CAPACITY

Two nagging issues are beginning to surface. Are there limits to future productivity? And are there are limits to future learning? And if so, are these issues correlated?

The value of evoking and projecting the law of diminishing returns is that it compels reexamination. Specifically, it requires the recognition and projection of increasingly diminishing gains. We may be going up a down escalator. In short, it may be time to sharpen the saw, except now it may have to be the softer and more speculative cutting edge of theory.

The title above is a good place to start because it is taken from a paper given by Howard Gardner, the Harvard educational and cognitive psychologist, to the American Educational Research Association on April 21, 2003. The paper was titled "Multiple Intelligences after Twenty Years." That double-paired focus on retrospect and prospect also might be just the sort of balancing act that institutions need to undertake now on behalf of the future.

There are eight intelligences identified by Gardner, which in turn had to survive eight criteria: linguistic, bodily kinesthetic, spatial, musical, logical-mathematical, intrapersonal, interpersonal, and naturalist. Two additional intelligences have been proposed: existentialist and futuristic.

Looking back to his seminal work *Frames of Mind* (1983) and reviewing his identification of eight multiple intelligences (MI), Gardner comes to a number of general conclusions that can be applied to the future focus of education and training.

All human beings possess multiple intelligences. The profile and range of intelligence dimensions vary with each individual. Multiple intelligences are the intellectual staples of the species. They are not synonymous with learning styles or talents. The former are externally mercurial and appear and disappear with social preferences and fashions. The latter are precious and distinctive gifts of special individuals but are not the common stock of the species.

Multiple intelligences describe all the basic and archetypal pathways the mind uses to learn. What determines which ones are used is a complex of three factors: genetics, experience, and societal priorities. Multiple intelligences rest on brain and genetic research. It is thus a process of describing and utilizing the basic learning pathways of the species. The brain is still being mapped. When completed it will be the equivalent of cracking the genetic code. The ultimate value of MI may be to serve as a major mainstay of a new science and art of mobilizing and measuring human potential.

Here are five critical checklist questions that educators, training leaders, and managers should ask as they review their current program array.

1. To what extent, if any, are any of current educational and training offerings based on multiple intelligences?
2. Are training goals and parameters typically narrow and short term and thus are prematurely constricting and limit stretching?
3. To what extent does training address how and not why, seek end results only, not source drivers?
4. How extensive, if at all, does training encourage multiple, alternative, and even divergent ways of exploring, communicating, and solving problems?
5. Finally, what does the totality of offerings say about the basic institutional assumptions of human potential and productivity? Limited or unlimited, circumscribed or yet to be tapped?

But even affirming the value of making a paradigm shift of thinking, learning, and leading (TLL), that still leaves the problem of implementation. What are the strategies for making it happen? The obvious approach is to employ Gardner's eight versions of MI as an overlay, note where it is lacking, and remedy the various sins of omission. But such add-ons perhaps should be put on hold until more basic spade work is done—until, in short, the list of learning processes is compiled that parallels and invites the learning pathways of MI. Such essential and recurrent processes common to all education and training would include communications, problem solving, interpersonal and intrapersonal relationships, decision making, innovation, and so forth. Let us use problem solving as an illustrative example.

As with all the above basic learning processes now under the aegis of MI, the starting point with problem solving is to characterize the process as essentially multiple in nature. That assumption, however, goes way beyond the externally oriented notion of the various tools in a tool box or arrows in a quiver.

MI initially engages not learning outcomes but pathways, not applications but first principles. It assumes the potential and power of all eight intelligences not only to engage but also to multiply problem definition. The goal, then, is to strengthen the problem solver by enriching the problem—to have it speak to the problem solver in a minimum of eight different languages, to make the problem increasingly multifaceted and more demanding.

Thus, in many ways, the initial gain of MI is to multiply access. Each intelligence becomes a learning pathway not only to the facade but also to the core of the problem. On the one hand, the extent of the impact of the problem is assessed and problem definition now spells out all that it can and may affect. On the other hand, MI approaches the problem as a functioning brain and probes its particular learning pathways in order to define what makes it a problem in the first place. Then, combining both external manifestations with internal dynamics, MI finally defines what state the problem has to acquire or how it has to be perceived for it to be no longer a problem.

The goal of problem solving then, as with all basic learning processes, is mutual enrichment, to tap the optimal taxonomy of human learning capacities. But that involves a double attribution. The first is the recognition that the value of MI is to extend learning range and depth. To be sure, according to Gardner, the cluster of MI selected and embraced by each individual is determined by genetics, experience, and societal preference.

But because problem solving itself and especially when driven by MI can both alter experience and be future driven, the potential for expanding the learning cluster is always available and can be tapped. In short, under the aegis of MI, the solution always involves stretching—it must always expand the range and depth of the problem solver. He or she should not be the same afterward. Growth gain not only should have expanded the range of productivity but also stirred the depth of MI potential. To work optimally, the process now has to be doubling—a win-win.

The first dimension of the problem-solving dynamic is thus primarily internal, but the second is external. MI has to be applied to the problem itself. The problem is now defined or redefined in terms of the eight intelligences. What determines its final version is what cluster sticks to it—that is, the equivalent of the problem's genetics, experience, and social preference. At its core is a problem and the extent of its impacts.

In other words, the problem-solving process has been transformed from a top-down, highly directive, and unilaterally controlling process to a collaborative mutually driven negotiating process. It is no longer a subject contemplating an object but two subjects contemplating each other. Moreover, each is now amplified—more substantial and challenging, more demanding of the other.

In many ways, the attribution of MI to the problem itself and the recognition that what finally adheres to it constitutes not only the learning identity of the problem but also establishes the threshold for its solution. The ideal is not the cry of "Eureka!" by the problem solver but the quiet capacity of the problem to solve itself. In fact, when and what the problem finally selects as its own operational multiple intelligence not only functions as its definition but also as its core and applications solution. The problem becomes self-solving. Its solution has about it an unarguable logic, clarity, and inevitability.

MI is thus a double-edged sword. It cuts both ways. On the one hand, it opens up the full range of learning pathways and the potential of being more than we are by virtue of learning more than we knew. It also enables learners to attribute to all the learning processes the same expansive array of intelligences. Such mutual attribution in fact changes the basic relationship between learner and what is learned. To borrow from Gardner, it aligns intrapersonal and interpersonal relationships and makes them not alternatives but versions of each other.

MI brings to training the science and art of realizing not only human but also process potential. It totally engages who we are, what we do, how we think, and how we problem solve. In the process, it also pushes the future forward—to all that we can be and all that we can do. But such gains always are mutual and reciprocal. They inevitably involve the species and its historical and evolutionary partners. It is no longer nature versus nurture but nature via nurture, and in the process it may grant training a new lease on life and perhaps a new future.

Finally, it clearly would be lamentable at this point in history to grant to machines greater potential for intelligence development than to human beings. What would make that also ironic is that bypassing or not tapping the optimal capacity of the human species, the future potential of machine intelligence would itself be impoverished.

What Gardner is essentially claiming is that composing a current obituary on the limits of learning and productivity is minimally premature and futuristically compromising. Indeed, training through MI has been given not only a new lease on current life but also a new future on stirring productivity and potential.

REFERENCES

Gardner, Howard. 1983. *Frames of mind: The theory of multiple intelligences.* New York: Basic Books.
———. 2003. *Multiple intelligences after twenty years.* Paper presented at the meeting of the American Educational Research Association on April 21.

19

MULTIPLE INTELLIGENCES AND HUMAN CAPITAL

Multiple intelligences (MI) is essentially involved in three generic tasks: problem solving, creativity, and accomplishing goals. So then, MI is analytical, intuitive, and purposeful. The process, however, is neither freewheeling nor totally self-determining. Goals provide a reality check. The problem posed or creative challenge is thus rooted in the real goals of a society or a work environment. In fact, such sanctioned goals energize, mobilize, and focus what intelligence responds to. In short, MI is at the service of society and its institutions and as such is an obedient agent of its goals.

The process of achieving such goals is enriched by tapping the multiple endowment of thinking, learning, and leading. But MI also invests communication and design with similar multiplicity. In these terms, the range of MI can be defined minimally as threefold: inquiry, communication, and application. MI is thus not only a way of knowing but also a way of communicating and shaping that knowing so that its happening fits. In other words, solutions produced and innovations created are never final. Rather, they represent the first step of a total, circular triadic process.

Inquiry is thus not enough. The solution or creation generated then must not only be communicated but also be shaped so that it can be integrated to function in the original environment that called it forth.

Supplementing inquiry also serves to test its validity. Indeed, communication and implementation are usually the agents and advocates of the goal-generating environment that triggered the process in the first place. As such, they function in the same way that a mission statement does: to determine congruence, alignment, and fidelity.

Perhaps a good example to demonstrate the total process is the decision-making process. Indeed, examining that process may kill two birds with the same stone: demonstrate what MI can contribute to decision making and how the MI tripartite process can be applied elsewhere as well.

MI functions as both the front and the back end of the decision-making process. Initially, it sets up, extends the range, and generates alternative decision options. The decision-making process is thus viewed as a problem-solving and/or creative challenge. Once the decision has been made, it then needs to be grilled in at least two ways: its capacities to be communicated and to survive implementation. At this end point, the full palette of MI is available to project and simulate the way the decision will be presented and perceived and what it will take to be wired in place with what already exists.

Such after-the-fact reflections position MI as an early warning or early opportunity process before the decision is officially promulgated. The implication is that if the decision fails to pass either or both tests of communication and implementation it goes back to the drawing board. But it is not back at square one because it now has the feedback data of communication and implementation as guidelines for revision.

But although it is clear what MI optimally can contribute to the formulation of a decision, why cannot the regular communications and management experts, unburdened with the baggage of MI, perform these same tasks and diagnose and catch problems before matters go too far? As already noted, they are rarely asked to do so. They are generally out of the decision-making loop. Decisions are made at the top and then promulgated. The difference with MI is that its involvement spans the entire process and thus in many ways grants it greater coherence. In other words, MI offers not only a different and perhaps better way of coming to decisions but also mandates a change in its post-decision dynamics. It imposes a circular structure that necessarily complicates the process and makes it more rigorous and multiply intelligent. Second, communication and implementation are not the same with MI as without it.

There are at least three kinds of transformation that MI offers to both communication and the implementation. First, as noted, it establishes a continuum. Both are now part of and an extension of the original inquiry and problem-solving and creative stage. No longer obedient, lesser-level lackeys word-smithing or engineering round pegs into square holes, communication and implementation are now an integral part of the problem-solving or innovation continuum. They now possess a power and importance that they have enjoyed before. Moreover, the performance standards are raised.

Second, good communication must now also be smart communication; the decision should bind people together, make them smarter, and build community. Affirmation and admiration of the company's intelligence should permeate the culture. Well-designed implementation must now be thoughtful; the decision should be durable, understandable, infallible, and flawless. It should appear afterwards as inevitable— as if it had always been there.

MI also enriches the number and kinds of options available to communication and implementation. Most obviously, it not only dramatizes what has been the dominant or favorite company mode but also extends and enhances it with secondary supportive intelligences. Thus, the preferred use of linguistic intelligence may be enriched by the spatial or even the musical, or even expressed through body language. Most important, the communication choices can be shaped by company demographics and their preferential modes of receptivity. The diversity of MI mirrors the diversity of the organization. In fact, MI typically is more comfortable with difference than with singularity. The ideal performance standard as noted then for MI communication is total access; for implementation, perfect fit.

The third and last contribution of MI is that it imparts unique and critical leverage to communication and implementation. If the communication of the decision, solution, or creative product encounters difficult, deflective, or distortive responses, or triggers an outpouring of dissatisfaction in areas not obviously or directly related to the issue being addressed, then the decision is put on hold. The same holds true for problems with implementation, hard or soft. If the application is incompatible with existing machinery or operations or if it is troublesome or dislocating (like inserting a square peg in a round hole), everything stops. In other words, the MI circular loop invests communication and implementation with veto power. They both become diagnostic trial runs. But all is not lost. The flawed decision is returned to its source but now freighted with what it now needs to incorporate communication and effective application. In some cases, the feedback insights may expose not just a flaw in the decision or solution but in the basic structure and mission of the company. In that instance, the reality check of MI may save the company.

But surely many CEOs and senior staff will object to such constraints on their leadership and executive decision making. After all, they might argue, certain decisions are not popular or easy to make or apply, but they are necessary and benefit the company. Yet every decision arrived at, every solution generated, every innovation that is produced by singular, nonintegrated, and discontinuous means and smarts may minimally be flawed and optimally not the best in class.

There thus may be two sins of omission: (1) The failure not to use MI to press inquiry to first or root causes or to x-ray the degree to which the problem is linked to more distant causes. The net result may be a solution that may house and pose a bigger problem in disguise. (2) To prevent decisions or solutions from falling between the cultural and operational cracks of the company, MI-driven follow-up and testing for weak spots functions as quality control. Smart communication and application catch and diagnose less-than-optimal solutions or decisions so that if the emperor has no clothes he will not be allowed to go out the door. If the original decision survives the gauntlet but benefits from testing the waters of communication and application, it will justify the extra steps.

The potential of human capital that MI embodies and offers organizations carries over to its operations as well. It is a new and rigorous way of raising expectations and performance standards on the one hand, and building culture, community, and best practices on the other. The ideal would be a MI-embedded learning organization.

EXECUTIVE COACHES AND TRUSTED ADVISORS: LEVERAGED INFLUENCE, LEADERSHIP PARANOIA, AND MBA GUIDANCE

Currently there are approximately 30,000 consultants in the United States generating about $50 billion annually. Of these, 10,000 are executive coaches, up from 2,000 in 1996. The number is increasing daily as a result of online training courses and entrepreneurs spreading the gospel at a fee of about $3,000 per person. Finally, there is the even more select and smaller group of trusted advisors retained by a select number of CEOs, heads of state, public personalities, elected officials, and similar executive positions. This group is estimated to range from 500 to 1,000 individuals but their impact far exceeds their numbers. In fact, it may be greater perhaps than all the consultants and executive coaches combined.

Who are these powers behind the scene and the throne? How did these advisors come to exercise such incredible leverage? What do these coaches have to offer that is so special, unique, and valued? What compels leaders to solicit their services? How are they used? What do these individuals have to offer that is not available from anyone else? Who are the members of this behind-the-scenes society of wise counselors who help leaders run the world with perhaps greater intelligence, wisdom, and caring than they would otherwise? How do these executive coaches and trusted advisors keep so many leaders on the straight and narrow and help to forestall the kinds of arrogant and often criminal activities that have characterized recent corporate meltdowns?

Answering these questions and telling the special stories of executive coaches and trusted advisors, especially the latter, is difficult because they are the tales of many who (like me) have taken vows of silence.

I have served as an executive coach and trusted advisor for more than 20 years. The past 10 years have been exclusively as a trusted advisor to a limited number of executive leaders. No one ever knew what I did or for whom; it had to remain hidden. I was like a secret agent. Although that is not all I did, I treasured that role and believe it offered as much fulfillment to me as it may have provided as much value to those whom I counseled.

But the role evolved over time. The challenges were never the same. The CEOs were always different. And, of course, I did not remain unaltered either. Indeed, constant and often unexpected personal and professional growth emerged as the first requirement of advisor. The notion of being experienced and even venerated was never enough. Indeed, one had to mirror the changes executives were compelled to make, including the difficulties of making them, if one was to understand even the language of the challenge, let alone help them cross the bridge— and in some cases, even build the bridge.

But what was absolutely clear is that the job, unlike any other, is temporary, invisible, and finally dispensable. No matter how critical the counseling may be at any time, the advisor must never lose sight of the fact that at best he (or she) is a sidebar, a wise whisper in the ear, a warning in the dark. He never can step forth out of the shadows into the light or speak in his own voice. He never can be the big cheese or the main event. At best, he is like the scaffolding erected on a building, necessary to help build it but once the edifice is complete, gone. Without such self-effacing denial, he is finished before he starts. Given the excessive egos of some executives, advisors frequently are tempted to urge similar self-restraint.

Another lesson that advisors frequently seek to impart, although it is often resisted, is fusing personal and professional change. Often it is not enough for the advisor just to offer a model of integration; he may have to spell out in explicit detail exactly the way it needs be done.

Many of my employers have questioned why personal and psychological change had to accompany a change in vision or direction of the company. Wasn't it enough that it had clear organizational benefits and gains? But for leaders that is never enough.

Behavior is the executive version of vision. Language is the lingua franca of direction and initiative. Attitude shapes problem solving. Curiosity makes decision making interesting. Standards drive the craft of implementation. In other words, what sets leaders apart from those who are not is that they have to live totally the life of their leadership.

They have to integrate who they are and what they do. They have to change themselves as they change the company. They can no more be the same afterward than the structures they have altered. They have to abandon the traditional separation that they can be one way at home and another at work. Rather, they have to become one, and all of a piece. Unexpectedly, both sides benefit and grow, symbiotically, and often both suffer equally.

Some executives believe they already have reached the apex. They often do not read any more. Many think they are such hot stuff that they pontificate. If they are surrounded by obedient and yes-man types, their principal collective function at times is to be called together is to serve as an appreciative audience or hallelujah chorus. Such CEOs always expect others to change, often and without question. But curiously they often exclude themselves from the process. Their top position gives them the illusion of finality.

As a devil's advocate, I remind them that top executives and leaders may or may not have been born, but they were always made—and constantly remade and on occasion even unmade. To claim perfection sets them apart in an unenviable way when one of their key functions is to demonstrate for emulation the highest standards—specifically, three.

1. *Integrity*. Which means no duplicity. They always have to be whole and of a piece. They have to not only generate solutions but also become and embody those solutions. The substance of each has to mirror each other and appear coincidental. It and they had been born at the same time.
2. *Communication*. They have to remember that they must always remain the supreme communicators. With authority, patience, and conviction they have to describe, explain, and justify a new direction so that it appears persuasive, compelling, and ultimately inevitable. They have to use whatever obstacles they personally have encountered to making the change, to helping others overcome resistance and reluctance. And above all, they have to use straight talk.

3. *Futurity*. They always have to picture and project the time after. They have to summon the future and position it in front of all so that whatever differences may have existed in the past or even the present, there now is a common future, shared and achievable by all. It is not enough to rally the troops and to give them their marching orders. The future has to become their leader. They also have to make others feel that it is all within their grasp. Outstanding leaders create leaders. That is their ultimate legacy.

Pretty heady stuff? A lot to lay on leaders? But as a trusted advisor, that is a norm. Otherwise it would to be touchy-feely stuff—happy, happy sessions high on flattery and cheerleading. And that was not what I and they were about.

The art of leadership counseling may find its ultimate value in becoming integral to leadership itself. Indeed, its final benefit may be to raise the bar on executive performance by recommending that the model of friendly opposition, upheld and embodied by their trusted advisors, be internalized.

Coaching executive paranoia is routine. Besides, as Saul Bellow's Herzog observes, "Just because I am paranoiac does not mean they are not really persecuting me." The favorite strategy of coaches is converting obstinate behaviors into flexible attitudes. Sometimes the results are significant and surprising.

What follows below is a leadership continuum that ranges from the manageable to the impossible (Bennis 1989) and that stakes out the challenges executive coaches regularly face.

NEUTRAL NORMS	WORST CASE EXAGGERATIONS
Difficult?	Impossible
Taxing?	Exhausting
Occasional?	Daily

Turned around by a persuasive advisor the result is counterbalancing mastery.

Discouraging?	Challenging
Overwhelming?	Energizing
Impasses?	Breakthroughs

And, the following guidelines and insights drawn from coaching can be added: leaders generally believe they are indispensable, refuse to acknowledge the limits of their job, can't admit that the job often consumes body and soul, turn to martyrdom as a frequent refuge, and expend superhuman efforts that generally fall short.

In the past, coaching, perhaps like traditional therapy, counseled acceptance. Leaders were encouraged to live with the demands of their jobs, and if possible reduce some of the excesses through delegation (Handy 1995). They were also urged to see and appreciate the upside— the achievements and the rush, respect, even admiration of those they lead. But for some perverse reasons, such consolation often did not work or last very long.

Why? It is such a sane approach. It blends knowledge of both the nature of the job with that of the client. But recurrent fears persist: not being equal to the challenges, surrounded by untrustworthy and even backstabbing associates, an incredible array of external forces and factors making success problematical if not impossible, and so on. The net result is frequent and urgent callbacks of coaches. The CEOs then spend their time venting and displaying their stigmata. Finally exhausted, the inevitable question surfaces: "What is wrong with me?"

INTRODUCTION OF PARANOIA

Typically, reassurance is offered but as noted fails. A new direction is to call the spade a shovel and to acknowledge paranoia as a norm: "The job is crazy and so are you. It is a mirror match. No divorce is possible. You have a tiger by the tail. Neither one of you will let go. It will never change its stripes. The only thing we can do is not hide or bury your paranoia because it goes with the job and with who you are. Instead, we have to bring it to the surface and start with accepting paranoia as a permanent tension, for you and your job. Then we have to find ways of making that paranoia work for you—making it protective, purposeful, and proactive instead of destructive, guilt-ridden, and draining."

I paused and waited. Then, I leaned over and in a softer, less assertive voice asked this one leader, "What do you think?"

The initial response was a deep breath. It was not a disapproving silence but thoughtful as if wrestling with a new complexity. Gradually, the leader came back to himself: "Well, I certainly did not expect that. I thought we would have a let-it-all-hang-out session followed by a pep talk and off I would go. But you stopped me in my tracks. Clearly, I am not comfortable about thinking about myself or my job in terms of paranoia. Then, too, if I am really going off the deep end, maybe I should go to a real shrink—no offense attended. But the problem with those guys is that they don't know about business and being a leader as you do. OK. What's the next step? Let's give paranoia a try."

Desperately buying time because I was not sure what the next step would be, I gave him an assignment: "For our next session I want you to think about and make a list of tasks that are daunting, people out to get you, and those on the sidelines cheering you on to failure. That is the first step of making your paranoia work for you. From that point on we will go further."

That experience turned out to be as much of a turning point for my coaching career as it may have for the leadership of many of my clients. As the methodology of paranoia took hold, major shifts occurred. The value of changing focus from resisting to embracing the limitations of the job, from believing that there is nothing wrong with you to recognizing the insightful nature of paranoia, was confirmed subsequently in sessions with a number of other leaders. And so my curious and perhaps dubious contribution to the voluminous literature of leadership has to do with coaching the development of protective, purposeful, and proactive paranoia for leaders.

What follows below is a record of a series of strategic conversations about typical executive paranoia expressed mostly in the form of questions. Often the questions exhibited a surprising capacity to be self-solving and informative.

THREE VERSIONS OF PARANOIA

Although coaching is generally problem and solution oriented, ideally both are provided by the mentee, not the mentor. But here things were different and even new. The client was puzzled. He or she was looking for guidance. The focus was doubly unfamiliar: not just paranoia but rather problem-finding and problem-solving paranoia. Structuring and stirring the muddy waters of paranoia creatively, three recurrent situations surfaced: threats, quandaries, and discontinuities.

Threats: Protective Paranoia

The coach began with paranoia basics. He asked his client to put together a list of threats. Typically, they included who is out to get me, who wants my job, who is undermining me and/or my company plans, what factions are forming or already exist, what is the rumor mill or grapevine saying about my leadership, what is my general standing with the rank and file, with stockholders, with board members, and on and on. Alongside the traditional to-do list, paranoia thus creates a to-worry-about list, ultimately perhaps more important than the first one (Rosen and Berger 1992).

Heeding paranoia and making it serve protective ends, the CEO finds he has to assign a higher priority to information gathering and, to follow the sage advice of the Godfather, "Keep your enemies close." A second major set of questions examines his assumptions about his key interpersonal relationships. Who will tell the emperor that he has no clothes? What has been his relationship with his senior staff? Has he surrounded himself with yes-men? Does he require constant approval with little or no dissent? Does he shoot the messenger? In short, has he inspired and developed "followship" (Sergiovanni 1984)? Has he created a team that will protect the quarterback from being blitzed (Block 1993)? Indirectly and ever so gently, the coach uses the occasion of threats to reexamine not only information networks but also executive interpersonal relations.

The advantage of operating from a base of paranoia is that threats can be accepted as a norm and not a personal leadership failing, and that once put in place, executive problem solving can be engaged. Thus, what the CEO needs to do is gradually wire in place an early warning or heads-up system. The internal intelligence gathering function should match that of the external monitoring of the market and the competition. Indeed, the first may feed into the second. Learning about internal capacity or the lack of it may directly affect market performance. Thus, surprisingly, worrying about threats may save not only his job but also his company.

Quandaries: Purposeful Paranoia

If one of the ultimate benefits of valuing paranoia is normalizing threats, another is relieving the CEO of the burden of always having to be Solomon. Expectations of being all knowing, all powerful, and all successful can lead to a false sense of indispensability. Paranoia does not make the CEO less needed, but it does argue that he or she may not be able to solve everything or be the only problem solver. The coach suggests the compilation of another list: What at work drives you crazy? What frustrates or compromises what you believe should be done?

At this point, the coach shifts gears. This dimension of paranoia requires a more reflective, thoughtful, and shared exchange. These are not direct threats with teeth bared as much as powerful enigmas that can cause sleepless nights and undermine companies at their core. And so the coach and the CEO together sustain an open-ended seminar on identifying and unraveling Gordian knots (Champy 1999).

Although many problems inevitably will surface, especially those nourished by ambiguity, the most difficult perhaps is how to bring about and persuade people to change. Even Senge (2004, 1990) recently confessed that his cherished learning organization in retrospect failed to alter fundamental attitudes and belief systems. Revisions in evolutionary theory by Gould (2001) and others using fossilized evidence suggest that species hang on tenaciously to who and what they are before allowing any change in the form of species splitting to occur. In other words, another generation may have to appear before there is real transformation. But that philosophical perspective may fail to silence the restlessness of paranoia or stop the determination of presidents to act presidential.

The CEO may be led to show a new interest in what the research may have to say on stirring change. Wisely, the coach focuses on egoless modes of organizational mechanisms and structures. So that change is welcomed, not required, and invited, not coerced, the coach introduces the approach of changing the outside as a way of changing the inside, and of shifting leadership from the vertical to the horizontal. In particular, the coach cites the notion of distributed leadership in which every employee's job description is rewritten to include a leadership component. Or Greenleaf's (1984) notion of rotational leadership of teams, based on the Roman legion's notion that leaders at best are *primus inter pares*. Or contemplating a less mechanical chart of organizational boxes and follow instead the more integrative and ecological design of Mitsubishi Electric, which fused divisions and functions into a more interactive seamless whole, based on the interconnected design of the rain forest (Kiuchi, 1997)—in short, shifting the focus from changing people to changing environments that change people.

Often what determines whether CEOs are closed or open to reengineering is their perception of whether it increases or diminishes the importance of their leadership. But nothing feeds the paranoia of failure as discontinuity (Buchen 2001).

Discontinuities: Proactive Paranoia

The high price paid for holding onto the past is that the future may abandon the organization. Instead, the coach and the CEO collaboratively try to engage the future, now. What surfaces are three villains: unacknowledged assumptions; singular not multiple forecasts and plans (Hamel and Prahalad 1994); the dissipation of coherence (Hammer and Champy 1993). Although all three are critical, the last brings everything full circle to square one where it all began.

The major issue has to become "What kind of leadership is required when discontinuity becomes a norm?" The CEO pulls back and is deep in thought, but unlike earlier discussions, the issue of leadership was in his comfort zone. Almost inevitably, his first overriding commitment is to fuse organizational mission and organizational leadership. In effect he made them one. He came to believe that he not only was in charge of the mission, but also its supreme advocate. At best he embodied it.

The fusion compelled him constantly to search for common and shared purposes. The past may offer some cherished older beliefs that still might have binding power, but vision will have to stretch for new sources of coherence in the future. He finally concluded that the principal task of the CEO is to bind both past and future together and to search for commonality.

The final paranoia was the harmony of time discords and of space continuums, of serving as prophet of science fiction. And curiously that taxing duality also made wearing two hats much easier, balanced, and almost respectable.

EDUCATIONAL COACHES

Coaches for MBA students may seem an expensive and questionable proposal. But one of the most intense pressures put upon all academics by adult learners and their employers is application of course content. That is neither new nor unjustified. And most instructors, institutions, and textbooks have acquitted themselves honorably and sometimes even creatively over the years: case studies are a norm, scenarios and simulations are assigned, collaborative team projects are often required, student chat rooms that feature workforce diversity are offered, and so on. But even such multiplicity does not seem to satisfy the current hunger for application, which has become stronger and more insistent, even strident.

What appears to be upping the ante? Of the many new pressures, an emerging one is minimal guidance. It is not unusual to have eight supervisors in as many months. And with outsourcing, sometimes with no supervisors at all, benign abandonment has become the norm. Then, too, even when available, mentors are stretched so thin, supervising more workers than ever before, that they have little or no time for individual coaching or counseling.

In short, course instruction is being asked to bear increasingly the double burden of mediating between a two-way flow: general application of course content not only to the workplace but also to the new and individualized operating realities of their employed students. Generic coverage can go only so far. It is just about able to manage the first task; not so the differentiated one. That requires a different and more creative solution.

The model suggested is supplemental, individualized, and optional. In addition to the instructor of record who has basic responsibility for delivering the course content, adult learners also should be offered academic coaches as an option for each course. Such coaches would not be required to hold the kind of terminal degrees that the course instructor must have. Rather, they are preeminent practitioners. They can be professional consultants and trainers, executive coaches, retired executives working for SCORE, alumni of the university, and similar individuals.

Profiles of each coach would need to be compiled and listed. Interested students would review and select the one who best matches their situation. They would pay a modest fee or honorarium. The exchanges would be maintained by e-mail and phone. All e-mail and written exchanges are copied to the instructor of record, who may occasionally join in the discussion.

The range of each coach needs to be both restricted and expansive. Although it does not include therapy, it can provide career guidance if requested. Coaches regularly might be requested to address the politics of the workplace. In some cases, it may have to be diversity specialized. It may have to focus on the special needs of women and minorities in the workplace. In such instances, clearly it would be helpful to select a coach who has encountered and surmounted such obstacles. Above all, the recurrent focus of coach and student is to apply the general approach and materials of the course to the specifics of the student's job and work environment. Finally, the hoped-for benefits of this kind of supportive and advocacy relationship will lead the student to consider adding coaching to his supervisory kit as he develops and advances in his own career. Who knows? He may even be involved in payback by serving later as an alumni course coach to a student.

REFERENCES

Bennis, W. 1989. *On becoming a leader*. Reading, Mass.: Addison-Wesley.

Block, Peter. 1993. *Stewardship: Choosing service over self-interest*. San Francisco: Berrett-Koehler.

Buchen, Irving. 2003. Employee mission statement. *PI* 40, no. 6: 40–42.

———. 2001. Disturbing the future. *Foresight* 4, no. 1: 36–42.

Champy, James. 1999. *Reengineering management*. New York: HarperCollins.

Greenleaf, Richard K. 1984. *Servant leadership*. Mahwah, N.J.: Paulist Press.

Gould, J. 1999. Fossil evolution. *Nature* 44, no. 3: 390–97.

Hamel, G., and C. K. Prahalad. 1994. *Competing for the future*. Boston, Mass.: Harvard Business School Press.

Hammer, Michael, and James Champy. 1993. *Reengineering the corporation: A manifesto for business revolution*. New York: HarperCollins.

Handy, C. 1995. *Beyond certainty: The changing worlds of organizations*. Boston, Mass.: Harvard Business School Press.

Kiuchi, Tachi. 1997. *Lessons from the rain forest*. Paper presented at the annual meeting of the World Future Society, San Francisco.

Ratcliffe, J. 2002. Scenario planning: Strategic interviews and conversations. *Foresight* 4, no. 1: 19–30.

Renesch, J. 1992. *Leadership in a new era*. San Francisco: Berrett-Koehler.

Rosen, Robert, and Lisa Berger. 1992. *The healthy company: Eight strategies to develop people, productivity, and profits*. New York: Putnam.

Senge, Peter. 2004. *Presence: Human purpose and the field of the future*. Cambridge, Mass.: SoL.

———. 1990. *The fifth discipline: The art and practice of the learning organization*. New York: Doubleday/Currency.

Sergiovanni, P. 1984. *Moral leadership*. San Francisco: Sage.

Van der Heijden, K. 1996. *Scenarios: The art of strategic conversations*. London: Wiley.

21

UNDERSTANDING AND
MULTIPLE PORTALS

Adaptability has increasingly become the key measure of performance. Recently a team of math experts found that students across the country—regardless of their good scores on standardized tests—do not really understand the basic concepts of math (*Education Week*, June 21, 2003, p. 34). Another survey concluded that top scores on high school graduation exit exams are not reliable predictors of college performance (*Education Week*, October 17, 2003, p. 14).

Nothing of such scale and invasiveness ever occurs in surveys of overall business training. Some industries will review the offerings of its members and even rate them by budget allocations and number of workshops. That is usually as far as it goes. To be sure, the introduction of learning management systems (LMS) has brought new precision and accountability to the entire enterprise. Most notably, not just the training but also its implementation has been pursued with vigor. But has it really?

In both educational surveys cited above, the failures were not of knowledge but of understanding. In turn, understanding is defined as mastery of a wider range of applications than taught. In other words, the students were unable to move beyond the original problem sets provided as part of initial instruction. They were stuck in programmed success.

Are the same limits operable in business training? Standard evaluations survey workshop clarity and relevance of presentation on the one hand, and implementation at the work site afterward on the other hand. But the applications may be prescriptive. The range of implementation similarly may be that of the workshop.

Employees may emerge knowledge rich but understanding poor. Their operational range may rest on a larger information base, but it is tied to a stake of limited and known applications. In short, they are compelled to be only prescriptively inventive. But knowledge and creativity need to be synergistically paired. Indeed, the ultimate application of understanding is innovation.

But perhaps the absence of such ambitious gains may not be perceived as a problem. After all, training always is targeted. It has limited goals. That limits the range of applications. If that range needs to be extended or redirected, another workshop can be created or the initial one extended or retooled. After all, is not that the way all education really operates—as progressively incremental? Then, too, the goal of understanding may be excessively egalitarian. Not everyone can be, has to be, or should be inventive. Perhaps that needs to be reserved for the talented. Doling out some knowledge is sufficient for most.

But the problem of innovation is across the board and its sources are not predictable. It emerges unexpectedly and from unlikely divisions or individuals. Besides, a number of arguments might be quickly advanced against forsaking the quest for understanding and settling instead for such mechanical and short-term incremental gains.

First, it costs more to mount more workshops rather than to conduct one thorough workshop. Second, the workplace is demanding more, not less, adaptability. Third, productivity gains are driven not by training but by workers reengineering their jobs. Fourth, higher not lesser expectations motivate. Fifth and finally, it is doable. Refocusing may be easier than imagined.

Reconfiguration requires changing the question from "How smart am I?" to "How am I smart?" Or better still, combine and routinely go back and forth between the two. Howard Gardner (1991) rightly suggests that double focus can best be accomplished by tapping brain research.

Advances in mapping the learning pathways of the brain have reached the point where the art may become the science of learning. In addition, cognitive psychologists are also beginning to link brain dynamics to the human genome and developing, no matter how tentatively, the genetic drivers of intelligence.

The net result is that we know more now about the way we think and the way we therefore learn than ever before. Human potential has thus become a less abstract and more precise and realizable target. Brain research may be providing educators and trainers with just the sort of leverage needed to address the intense realties of the work place on the one hand, and to offer optimum understanding and adaptability on the other. Moreover, brain research may overcome reluctance by serving as an overlay rather than an overhaul. That way the baby is not thrown out with the bath water, and professionals have a way of testing before changing.

The goal of the overlay is to pair understanding and adaptability. It is not enough to simply know. Because it is more difficult and important to understand than to know, we tend to favor knowledge over understanding. That preference is shored up by the way we test on the one hand and the way we measure application on the other.

But the brain values total competence and confidence. The brain welcomes being stretched rather than just confirmed. The brain wants to experience and affirm its power and be endlessly enriched. The brain, in short, is always hungry. Feeding and stirring the brain always requires upping the ante. And it seeks all this from the start.

The overlay provided below is for completeness. Although each level of each of the three basic operating principles is correlated, only the last triad is the focus here:

1. Progressive Mastery:
   Information
   Knowledge
   Understanding
2. Adaptability Range:
   Explicitly identified (known problem sets)
   Broadened base (stretched)
   Crossovers (innovative and discoverable)
3. Entry Portals (Instructional Frames) and Exit Portals (Applications):
   Singular (rote and ritual)
   Varied but discrete (diversity and learning styles)
   Multiple and interoperable (intelligence and the range of applications)

The discussion here will center on the portals. Hopefully, that will also serve to shed light and serve as a further commentary on understanding and crossover.

The selection of portals rests on the assumption that the way training begins determines whether or not understanding and optimum adaptability occurs. Entry thus drives outcome. Beginnings determine ends. Each portal has to be properly framed to be optimized.

The framework selected has to permit and accommodate the criteria of access and range. It therefore must be multiple, not singular, in nature. It also must raise the bar and extend the range of applicability. It should always resist closure or finality but remain open ended and unfinished. Finally, although given here in full, the portals form a menu for selection. Not all need be used for any given workshop.

The basic problem Gardner raises is that of singularity: one teacher, one trainer, one textbook, and one curriculum for many different students. His familiar argument is that learning styles vary considerably and no teacher can be 360 degrees, especially with an unfavorable teacher-student ratio. His solution is to provide multiple learning approaches or his famous eight multiple intelligences. That provides a congenial series of learning styles from which students can select their preferred way into a mandated curriculum.

The dynamic offered by Gardner rests on a number of instructional assumptions. The instructor realizes the limits of his or her range and shifts the focus from the server to the menu. The student is not passive but has to be cooperatively engaged in trying out and finally selecting his or her preferred learning style, from which innovation will come or not. The goal of individualizing instruction is to serve as an antidote to stereotypical learning and thinking. Above all, the dynamic establishes the goals of training as real understanding and optimum adaptability.

The use of multiple portals or entry points sets up and enhances the varied avenues to reach those goals. At least seven portals are available: narrational, historical, foundational, psychological, quantitative, esthetic, and futuristic.

To demonstrate how each of the above can be incorporated or built into training, a workshop focused on employee evaluation will be used as illustrative. Each portal will be followed by two paired descriptors: entry mode and intelligence choice.

I. NARRATIONAL

Simulation   *Verbal and Linguistic Intelligence*
The value of story especially at the outset is that it establishes the
complexity of reality. It simulates real life, issues, and people. It persua-
sively builds credibility. It may be verbal or visual or, better still, both. If
it is also humorous, that is a plus, not an essential.

> One company I worked for ran an office betting pool. One had to do with the
> longest period between evaluations. The winner was 28 years. The other was
> on the oddest place for an evaluation to take place. The winner was standing
> in line together at the airport. What does that tells us about evaluation?

2. HISTORICAL

Reflection   *Evaluative Intelligence*
History invites reflection. Evaluation is not perceived as a one-shot or
static or nondevelopmental process. Above all, a historical perspective
suggests that what is being discussed is purposeful and consciously designed to fulfill certain goals.

> In the 19th century, evaluation was generally hurried and crude. Workers
> were hands, and owners were heads. Dickens portrayed the school exit as
> being the same as the entrance of the factory. Although there were many
> changes and refinements in the 20th century, evaluation remained the in-
> contestable realm of the boss. But as unions took hold and productivity
> became an increasingly important factor, metrics and continuous im-
> provement emerged. Assessment was driven to a large extent by Deming's
> statistical process controls, which transformed evaluation into measurable
> performance improvement. What changes have you observed over the
> years? What are some other changes that may occur in the future?

3. FOUNDATIONAL

Speculation   *Assumptions Intelligence*
The value of the foundational or philosophical framework is to stir speculation. History addresses how, philosophy why. It invites an attention to
first causes or square-one thinking.

Evaluation seems built into us. We always want to know how we are doing. Even God in Genesis steps back after one of his daily creations to determine that it was good. Imagine if he didn't like it. After all, he may have regretted creating us. So whatever we are, we are also and always evaluating creatures. Describe some ways other than work in which we are always testing and measuring things and people to see if they pass muster.

4. PSYCHOLOGICAL

Intrapersonal and Interpersonal Self-Analysis   Emotional Intelligence
The psychological dimension introduces the ambiguity of evaluation—the degree to which we are pulled toward and away from it at the same time. It compels us to look inwardly at our feelings and points outwardly at our relationships. It presents evaluation as a complex psychological dynamic that reaches into our deepest emotions and fears and extends to how we relate to others. Above all, it defines psychology as form of knowing.

We started out and set the stage by presenting and explaining why an evaluation could be postponed for so long or why it could occur in the unlikely place of a line at the airport. But now let us try to push that further. I need four volunteers. Two will pair off and play the role of a supervisor and employee in an evaluation situation. They do not have to improvise. I have written the script. You just read your part. The other two will play the same roles, but they will express out loud the thoughts and feelings going through the minds of each after each exchange. If anyone in the class believes you are holding back or deflecting, he is free to fill in what should be expressed.

5. QUANTITATIVE

Sizing, Scaling, and Estimating   Math Intelligence
Everything is measurable. It helps however to make it manageable—to get a grip on it. Numbers always help. So does taking an abstract idea and making it visible—like picturing justice as blindfolded and holding a scale. Evaluation is no exception.

What percentage of the total budget is earmarked for employee salaries? For benefits? For training like this workshop? OK, while we are at it, let us also try to quantify something qualitative. How much time do you spend typically each year in evaluation sessions and formal training? Take CD-ROM workshops at home? Personal training on your own: reading work-related books and articles, listening to tapes? Finally, estimate how much time a supervisor typically spends on evaluation. Because undoubtedly the final totals will range, let us ask for three volunteers to put their numbers on the board up front.

6. AESTHETIC

Shape and Design   *Spatial Intelligence*
All things are shaped to serve a double master: form and function. In addition, things are not just put in place. They have to fit. Square pegs in square holes. They have to line up with what goes before and what comes after. Engineers generally understand this—that is why placemats exist to make drawings—and human engineers have to understand it more. Above all, access and equity have to partner. One design does not fit all. "One law for the lion and ox is oppression" (William Blake). Worse, it is also inefficient.

We already noted the historical changes in evaluation. Let us look at evaluation as a design problem. First off, should the system be totally uniform? Should it be adjusted for different departments? If so, how and why? Let's explore differentiated design.

7. FUTURISTIC

Anticipatory and Change-Driven   *Visioning and "What If" Intelligence*
This is not planning—that is a separate and different process, although visioning ideally should precede and inform it. The futuristic is poised for change. It compulsively entertains different, better, faster, and cheaper ways of doing the same old thing the same way. The future and productivity mutually support each other as natural partners. In fact, the purpose of emphasizing the future is to perceive it as an ally, not an enemy,

To what extent is the present evaluation system current and up with the times? Is it cutting edge? If not, what changes do you envision being made? Let's take another futuristic tack. To what extent is the present performance improvement system time-bound? It leaves out the future—your future and the future of your job. Let's take a few minutes to write a future job description—of what our job would look like two or three years down the pike. And then itemize what training you would need to get there.

SUMMARY

The following matrix provides a summary of all seven portals, their preferred modes of thought, the kinds of intelligence featured, and the growth gains.

Portal	Mode	Intelligence	Gains
1. Narrational	Simulation	Verbal/Linguistic	Memorization
2. Historical	Reflection	Evaluative	Perspective
3. Foundational	Speculation	Assumptions	First Causes
4. Psychological	Self-Analysis	Emotional	Work Dynamics
5. Quantitative	Scaling	Math	Problem Measurement
6. Aesthetic	Design	Spatial	Form/Function Fit
7. Futuristic	Anticipation	"What If"	Visioning

Will understanding and optimum adaptability eventually and always follow? Not always and certainly not immediately. But training with multiple portals is an investment and a seeding process. It operates on the premise of all brain research: the expanded definition and range of human potential, and the infallible relationship between understanding and optimum adaptability.

Besides, even if all seven portals were selected, such beginnings would take very little time as noted above. They might even make workshops less routine and predictable. Most important, attendees would be engaged in a muscular way from the start. It is, after all, an overlay not an overhaul. And that may turn out to be enough to surprise employees into being creative.

REFERENCE

Gardner, Howard. 1991. *The unschooled mind: How children think and how schools should teach*. New York: Basic Books.

22

DIAGNOSTICALLY DRIVEN TRAINING

The current process of selecting training topics focuses essentially on what the company believes it and its employees need to succeed together. Relatively little attention is paid to the cognitive psychology of employees, their intrapersonal and interpersonal receptivity, or the range, actual and potential, of their intelligence to grasp and implement the training. The current emphasis on e-learning technology and cost savings deals mostly with the externals of training. It generally leaves untouched assessing and defining the capacity of those trained to contribute to their training.

In other words, training may be guilty of the old myopia of focusing on the business rather than on the customer. Instead, it needs to balance what it is offering with how it is being perceived and received. That also would happily accommodate a shift from the evaluation of the training and its implementation to the transformation of the employee trained. Such a focus would include another implementation evaluation too often also ignored or unassessed: the degree to which the training is internalized, the extent to which not only the work changes productively but also the employee is altered habitually. In short, training needs to be preceded, shaped, and driven by employee data. It needs to be targeted.

Happily, some diagnostic tools—at least three—are available. One is traditional, a second recently updated, and the third innovative. Training has to catch up and be driven minimally by the diagnostics of how we sell and serve (marketing), how we relate (human resources dynamics), and how we think (cognitive psychology). The first, although tried and proven, generally has been untapped or applied to training design. The second, Myers-Briggs, recently has been updated and focused on team building. The third, multiple intelligence, although around for more than 20 years, has only recently captured the attention of instructional designers in business. In other words, the state of the art of creating leaning management systems (LMS) can be advanced by also creating the state of the art of learning management diagnostics (LMD).

Training could benefit immediately, significantly, and obviously from the external and extensive knowledge of customer and market behaviors. Every training program should employ the overlay of customer knowledge and service. Whatever the specific training subject, the customer would be a recurrent, almost obsessive, generic focus. Regardless of job title, job description, or customer proximity, every employee would have in front of him or her a dynamic profile of customers using the company's product or service. The principal form that dynamic profile would take is that of simulation, especially enhanced by role-playing and storytelling. Indeed, the combination of the three generally has been found to be the most effective mode of communication and training. They even have proved to be invaluable in testing new products and services in terms of customer appeal and purchase. All training would thus feature the demographics and sociology of marketing to the extent that every employee in every training program would be customer driven.

Another key diagnostic that has been used by human resources for quite some time is a series of psychological assessment tools. These include the well-known Myers-Briggs, Strong Personal Inventory, Thomas-Kilman Conflict Mode Instrument, and similar instruments. They are generally employed externally as part of an initial recruitment screening of applicants as well as occasionally internally for purposes of determining or testing for promotion or leadership positions. But, strangely, they generally have not been applied to training, until recently.

CCP (formerly Consulting Psychologist Press), a major provider of the basic assessment tools, has developed the MBTI (Myers-Briggs Type Indicator) Team Building Program. The concept is to administer MBTI to each team member and thereby to generate the preferences and profiles of the entire team. (That also must include the team leader, who often seeks to solidify his role as the team manipulator by not taking the test.) So armed and informed, communication and teamwork can be improved, and the negotiation and resolution of conflicts and differences can be made more manageable. Once again, the gain is twofold and synergetic: both the work process and the worker, by being more closely aligned with task and team dynamics, enjoy greater productivity. The adage of working smarter rather than harder finds perhaps its major advocate in such diagnostically driven training.

The third tool is seldom used and generally has not been applied to training design. It is multiple intelligences (MI) developed by Howard Gardner of Harvard and presented initially in his book *Frames of Mind* (1983). Gardner basically argued that intelligence is neither confined to nor measurable by only one intelligence (the literacy of reading and writing). Rather, there are many intelligences. He originally designated seven, then added an eighth in 1993. Although originally and subsequently mostly taken up by educators and school textbook publishers, MI has the potential by itself, and especially allied with the other two, to offer the most powerful and impactful training diagnostic available today to business. Its ambitious reach was announced recently by Gardner in a 20-year retrospective.

Gardner claims there are eight intelligences: linguistic, bodily, spatial, musical, mathematical, intrapersonal, interpersonal, and naturalist. Equally as important, MI is trackable and traceable as the basic learning pathways of the brain. In fact, when cognitive researchers complete their total mapping of the brain, the results and applications may rival that of cracking the genetic code. But the critical point for the discussion here is the fusion of physiology (brain) and psychology (cognition). Linking human thinking and learning, Gardner claims that MI characterizes not just individual or social behaviors but those of the human species itself. In other words, MI goes way beyond learning styles or preferences and even natural or developed gifts or talents. It also transcends historical differentiation. It is what all humans possess by virtue of being human. Indeed, that starting point enables Gardner to present the general operating laws of MI that may also be those of training as well.

The range of MI varies with each individual. The extent and depth of that range is determined by genetics, environment, and use. The range of MI is not fixed or predetermined. It can be expanded by education, exposure, and direction. Goals and environment can guide, stimulate, and even determine the configuration of intelligences chosen or favored. But control is never total because MI autonomously operates with a mischievous will and direction of its own.

For goals to be optimal, they should always combine the small and the big, the immediate and the long term. MI is brought more fully into play, mobilized, and energized by task completion and task extension, accomplishment, and incompletion. MI is also stirred when the focus is on "uncovering" rather than "covering" materials or topics. Basic ideas and concepts—square-one thinking or first-cause thinking—stimulate the synergistic interplay between MI and problem solving. It is particularly responsive to the multiple challenges of constructing scenarios, simulations, case studies, portfolios, and so forth—in short, to artificial and futuristic realities.

Finally, the ultimate value of MI may be to serve in Gardner's terms as "the optimal taxonomy of human capacities" (2003).

To many, the above may appear too academic and removed from the urgencies of training to have any practical value. But perhaps MI can become less distant but still remain challenging if it is perceived not only as a new way of revisiting human potential but also a series of multiple smarts. What Gardner is really saying is that as a species we always exceed at any given point in time the definition of who we are, what we know, and what we can learn. There is thus a need to tap and direct each of the eight intelligences so that they are rendered and extended in terms of immediate growth and long-term expectation.

What may be further helpful is to translate and animate multiple intelligences into action applications. Thus, each MI respectively could be rendered as follows: word smart, body movement adept, spatially agile, musically facile, math sequenced, personally and interpersonally savvy, and environmentally sensitive. In addition, clustering preserves and enriches the dynamics of the process. Operationally, one intelligence may dominate, but it often taps or engages others in a support capacity to address a task or solve a problem. The process thus features primary, secondary, and even tertiary intelligences all activated by the nature and complexity of the task on the one hand, and the interactivity of smarts of the problem solver on the other. Indeed, the more formidable or unfamiliar the challenge, the more resourceful and varied the team of intelligences marshaled. To be sure, an important and recurrent goal of training is to enlarge and differentiate the range of tools in the toolbox. But the key first step of diagnostics still has to be taken.

Every employee needs to be assessed as to his or her MI range and potential. To tie together improvement potential of both work and worker, the assessment also should be linked and ultimately made part of job description. Such data would then be used not only to shape the design of training but also to benchmark growth and realization of potential. Training design also should factor in Gardner's key guidelines for optimum stimulation and synergy noted above. In other words, training design would always incorporate immediate and long-term goals, be intellectually rigorous, focus on governing ideas and first causes, be practical and visionary, and offer the multiple challenges of simulation and scenario.

Such a revised and enlarged scope of training would yield outcomes that are both work and worker specific. What is done better would always be fused with what in fact drives such improvement: the application not only of more intelligence but also of more intelligences. Suddenly, productivity would no longer be limited to a singular or narrow definition of the work task or process, and workers themselves would no longer be confined to what they have been or what they use. By tying together productivity and human potential, trainers may be able to tap a whole new vein of learning. Becoming smarter may become not only longitudinal but also holistic. In short, MI may be able to offer more of the future at the service of the present than ever before.

REFERENCES

Gardner, Howard. 1983. *Frames of mind: The theory of multiple intelligences*. New York: Basic Books.
———. 2003. *Multiple intelligences after twenty years*. Paper presented at the meeting of the American Educational Research Association on April 21.

23

MULTIPLE INTELLIGENCES APPLICATION: LEARNING SUCCESS CENTER

Increasingly, professional trainers and corporate universities are recognizing and tapping the contribution of diagnostically driven training to increasing productivity and innovation. What do the diagnostics yield? A series of employee profiles that displays both individual and group learning preferences, relationships, styles, and talents. They range from the emotional and psychological to the conceptual and cognitive. What new dimensions appear? Minimally, three new linkages:

- Who we are and how we relate are also how we learn.
- How we team is how we learn collaboratively.
- "How smart am I?" becomes "How am I smart?"

What tests should be administered? Three types:

1. Psychological: Goleman's Emotional Intelligence and Myers-Briggs
2. Team-related: MBTI (team adapted) and Belbin's Team Behaviors
3. Cognitive: Gardner's Multiple Intelligences

Key assumptions of constituent expectations and benefits:

1. Students: Increased self-knowledge of personal, collective, and cognitive dimensions and how they can be applied to improved learning success and career crossover.
2. Faculty: Increased awareness and precise knowledge of the range and difference of their students and how such profiles can lead not only to more targeted assignments, team projects, and student participation, but also to more overall, effectively inclusive, instruction.
3. Staff: More knowledgeable advising, counseling, and guidance.
4. Institution: Increased student retention.

APPLICATION

All incoming students would be offered on an optional basis a unique no-cost service: an opportunity to profile their learning performance styles and potential by taking a series of diagnostics (currently without charge on the Internet). Such a profile also would apply to work and career pathing. A copy of the profile would be offered to each student in three forms: just data; an interpretive overlay, available and constructed online; and a scheduled scripted session with a learning success counselor.

To provide assurances of privacy, all data provided by students from questionnaires will be erased. All that remain will be the profile. Access to the profile will be password protected. In effect, each student will be diagnostically empowered. Increased self-knowledge will raise students' learning success levels, increase and improve their special contributions to course discussion, optimize their participation in team assignments, and structure their future goals.

For faculty, the profile would be accompanied by an explanation of the various adaptations instructors could employ to match more precisely the learning processes with individual strengths, and build in appropriate stretch gains. The profile would guide faculty responses and choices of individual and team assignments. In addition, students can indicate to instructors at the outset a series of growth goals in all three areas. At the end of the term, both students and faculty will record comments that document or redirect the learning profile to those chosen and to other future goals and applications. Sessions with learning success counselors would be profile guided and provide stronger databased course selection and expectations.

BENEFITS

- *For students*: projection of learning strengths to enhance both academic and career performance.
- *For faculty*: precise ways of tapping and adjusting assignments and team collaboration to the range of student profiles.
- *For staff*: development of detailed academic and career growth plans.
- *For the institution*: significant additional way of securing retention while offering a unique positioning and marketing message setting the institution apart from the competition.

NEXT STEPS

Creating a learning success center (LSC) would coordinate and subsume learning success activities of all schools. Heads and staff directors of each school would constitute the steering and advising committee.

The initial agenda of LSC would be:

- Identifying the tests, formats, and protocols.
- Designing a student self-administered profile applications kit.
- Develop and communicate course and faculty applications of profiles.
- Ditto staff applications.
- Benchmark students admitted under this new service and set up monitoring system to determine change, if any, in retention rates.

Thus, the inclusive nature of MI would enrich and extend learning success.

24

THE MULTIMODAL
JOURNEY OF MANAGERS

Whatever external challenges current managers face, nothing compares to those that directly have affected their basic managerial roles and tasks. They now have to supervise more employees, plug holes caused by downsizing, compensate for workers who often do not have the required work skills, and face many similar challenging tasks. In addition, there has been a steady erosion of their authority and control. In many plants, teams have taken over. They virtually do everything that mangers previously did. The net result is that managers have become almost superfluous in some instances.

Managers are also finding their knowledge base eroding. New and rapid emerging redefinitions of and demands on their jobs confront them daily: reengineering, balanced score card, employee mission statements and universities, collaborative work covenants, learning organizations, and so on. In short, how does one bring forth a new manager, phoenix fashion, out of the ashes of multiple crises and dislocations?

The focus would have to be on transition and reflection and, above all, reflection about transition. One of the hoped-for double outcomes would be the gradual acceptance of reflection as a habitual practice and of transition as a new norm of reality. The rites of a passage to accomplish both goals require identifying three archetypal metaphors to engage both reflection and transition.

One is the figure of Janus, the second of branch points, and the third the learning journey. Janus addresses time; branch points, space; the learning journey, process and linkage.

Appropriately, the figure of Janus, whose name is reflected in the pivotal month of January, sets up the Janerian duality of past and future, retrospect and prospect, genesis and terminus. The past provides benchmarking, the future capacity for anticipating.

The other metaphor is equally powerful. Its classic expression perhaps appears in the lines of Robert Frost: "Two roads diverged in the woods, and I—/I took the one less traveled by/And that has made all the difference" (1969, 105). The archetype of choice is not only comprehensive but also recurrent. A choice is not made once and for all time. The road not taken is offered again and again.

Then, too, choice is not limited to externals like lifestyle, career, or calling. It also includes our preferred ways of perceiving, conceptualizing, structuring thought, problem solving, decision making, and so forth. In short, it is a complex and alternative identity as rich and different perhaps as the one chosen.

When the metaphors of Janus and branch points are joined, they support in reinforcing manner a third archetype—that of the learning journey. How do we come to know what we know? How do we develop the assumptions that drive unknowingly so many of our decisions and judgments? What is our relationship to the past and the future? What choices did we make, when, and why? And what are the choices before us?

It is not always easy to reconstruct our learning journey because earlier ideas have often been left behind. They are also not perceived as a lamentable loss. They usually occurred at a formative period when we were still unfinished and not fully educated or acclimated into a career or work-think. Thus, whatever and wherever we were at any given point in time was always in the process of being revised, retrained, upgraded, and transformed into something so far superior that the old self and its old ways were not worth keeping alive and current.

In any case, what was displaced was regarded for the most part as inferior or inadequate. It served its purpose up to that point but was then cast aside and generally was not available to us any more. It is not unlike the basic difference between science and literature. Science does not have to be cumulative; culture does.

As new perspectives are gained, others are discarded. The learning journey involves an endless and inevitable series of trade-offs. In times of intense change, development may be accelerated and occur with greater discontinuity, just as organizational structures are sometimes altered drastically or reengineered. When that occurs often or deeply, the effect may be unsettling.

Managers may be totally unsure of what they are supposed to be and do, just as companies may be confused as to their direction. When things become bewildering, it is perhaps necessary to step back and, above all, look back. That in turn requires adopting the dual directions of Janus, retrospect and prospect, reflection and anticipation.

In the process, it may be helpful for managers to reflect back on and benchmark change—professional and organizational—at every stage of their development. In essence, managers inevitably reflect upon their learning journey, which is their individual version of transition. In other words, the learning journey brings together and subsumes the double perspective of Janus, retrospect and prospect, and the ritual drama of making choices—and does so in an extensive reflective review of learning branch points and transitions. It is to the review of the journey that managers need to turn to find both their new and the affirmation of their traditional roles.

THE LEARNING JOURNEY

When managers recall their past education, training, and experience, what frequently emerges is how much the role of the manager itself has dramatically altered over the years, and how sometimes they are not happy with the results. For example, many managers were initially given the textbook definition of the five roles of the manager: planning, organizing, staffing, leading, and controlling.

What many found over time is that leading and controlling were altered dramatically. They were called upon to motivate more than lead or to lead by motivating. Control increasingly was eroded by employee empowerment. The dominance of teams meant that singular control of hiring and firing now had to be shared, especially if HR was outsourced. Follow-up became an increasingly bigger part of planning, especially following up the implementation of training. Above all, because of the increasing emphasis on productivity, performance appraisal became performance improvement. It was the manager's responsibility now as facilitator or coach to bring about that transformation and in the process align employee with business stretch goals.

If one were to compare the job description of managers when they started out with their current versions, it might appear as if they were talking about two different positions altogether. But that is precisely the value of retrospective reflection. Indeed, there are at least three benefits conferred by the learning journey of transition.

YIELDS OF THE LEARNING JOURNEY

1. *Documentation*. Recording over time the evolutionary history of the job of manager and learning choices. Changes did not just happen. They involved branch points—roads taken and not taken. In the process, new understandings and perspectives are acquired.
2. *Unlearning*. On a very direct and personal level, managers recognize the degree to which a learning organization also has to become an unlearning organization in order to be effective.
3. *Celebrations of Survival and Change*. Valuing resiliency, persistence, and agility as affirmative. The manger emerges as a survivor of many wars. He also learns to lead and be an advocate of innovative change. He helps to initiate and sustain debate about changing managerial roles. He entertains job and even career change, including going abroad where traditional managers may be more highly valued. Finally, he projects alternative organizational futures that may serve to recover and pursue new lost opportunities and earlier roads not taken.

The common denominator of all of the above is to bring the learning review to the threshold of the future. It is at this point where the question of what lies ahead for managers generates his unfinished agenda. The process of retroactively evaluating past solutions or interventions against the realities they were supposed to address may uncover or recover alternative innovations suggested earlier by managers but that, like the road not taken, never saw the light of day. The process of future-facing thus recaptures lost opportunities in the past. It is like leapfrog-ging—while we are getting ahead, let us also catch up.

Standing at the Janerian threshold where the past and the future con-verge also provides managers with the illusion of a blank slate. They may wish to speculate on not only what mangers are likely to be but also what they ideally should be. For a change, they might like to design their own jobs rather than having it always done for or to them. In the process, they probably also would have to identify what they need to learn to get from the present to the future. And so appropriately the final yield of the learning inventory may be the training agenda of the future.

In summary, then, the learning journey that focuses on the perma-nence of transition offers much. The journey brings a probing and self-conscious intelligence to bear on the trajectory of education and train-ing; raises to the level of conscious review, perhaps for the first time, assumptions that drive decisions; and compels an insightful interplay be-tween the past, present, and the future. In many ways, it can serve to structure midlife career change and to provide the rites of passage to re-new and restore balance in the future. It can create out of managed tur-bulence a more informed, innovative, and proactive professional—a manager of transition, ad infinitum. Finally, as noted often, multiple in-telligences is itself a metaphor that transcends whether the various in-telligences are tapped. It can also serve as a rich model of creative prob-lem solving. MI is always and already out-of-the-box.

The last outcome brings the learning review smack up against the fu-ture and the need to anticipate it. It is at this point where what lies ahead generates the unfinished agenda. The evaluation of past solutions or interventions against the realities they were supposed to address may recover and underscore innovative notions or creative problem-solving techniques suggested by managers along the way but which for various reasons never took hold or were tried out. Standing at the Janerian threshold where the past and future converge, mangers may wish to en-joy the luxury of speculating on what a manager and an organization ide-ally should be in the future, and where both have fallen short in the past. Finally, because these regrets also may be more global than what sur-faced in the series of outcomes noted above, they may even be more provocative—that is, appropriately futuristic.

In summary, then, the value of the learning inventory lies in the urgent intelligence that is brought to bear, in raising to the level of conscious review assumptions that drive decisions, and compelling an insightful interplay between the past, the present, and the future. In many ways, it is a structured and revealing midlife crisis designed to create or restore balance for the future. It generates renewal and recommitment as a more informed and proactive professional. Undertaken company wide, it can give organizations new vitality, direction, and purpose.

At the end of Mark Twain's *The Adventures of Huckleberry Finn*, our young hero, after reviewing his many escapades, is not content just to hang around but instead yearns "to light out for the territory ahead" (1989, 294). For Huck that was the lure of the West. It was also the promise of the future. For America it was both. This country has always had a love affair with what lies ahead. Now there is also the need to find ways of reconfiguring the branch points for its managers of the future.

REFERENCES

Frost, Robert. 1969. *The Poetry of Robert Frost: The Complete Poems, Complete and Unabridged*. Edited by Edward C. Latham. New York: Henry Holt.
Twain, Mark. 1989. *The Adventures of Huckleberry Finn*. New York: Tom Doherty. (Originally published 1884.)

25

BUSINESS APPLICATIONS OF MULTIPLE INTELLIGENCES

Although corporate smarts are highly valued, the general impact of multiple intelligences on the business sector in general and human resources has been minimal. A few consultants have suggested applications to training and leadership (Martin 2001; Riggio, Murphy, and Pirozzolo 2002). Even a quick review of HR assessment tools reveals that only the old war horses of Myers-Briggs and personality inventories like those of Strong are still around and generally all that is used. No major training programs or learning management system (LMS) show any signs of tapping into MI, let alone reconfiguring the extensive menu of offerings accordingly.

Speculation as to why MI generally has been ignored by business yields three possible answers. The first two are characteristically short-sighted, even snobbish; the third, substantive. First, MI's origins are academic. Gardner was advancing theory, not application; research, not conclusive findings. His primary audience was other psychologists. Then, too, although the criteria developed for determining both the range and operations of each intelligence appeared to be so rigorous and comprehensive and its results definitive, the absolute nature of the original seven shortly was shaken by the emergence of an eighth and now by the contemplation of a ninth and even a tenth. The effect in

some circles was akin to adding additional commandments to the original ten. The issue of what the final number would be suggested to
many that the research was still an ongoing academic inquiry.

Second, because MI began to partner primarily or only with education, distancing by business occurred. Indeed, that linkage confirmed its
lineage: this was basically an academic taxonomy designed for teachers
and schools. And as the number of books and articles proliferated, and
as the curricula and staff development adaptations began to surface, MI
appeared to have found its place and advocates. Given the typical de-
valuation of education by business, many corporate practitioners concluded that guilt by association once more was operative.

Third, MI seems to be at variance historically with the dominant
thought patterns. After all, it originally was presented and subsequently
proliferated in book form, and literacy is still the principal form of
thought and expression. It has been debated whether MI is merely a
more ambitious version of learning styles or the traditional exceptional-
ity of talent or gifts possessed by a relatively few lucky individuals. Finally, multiple intelligences appeared to be unmanageable. There are
too many, the range was bewildering, the way they internally interact
still a mystery, and so on. In short, perhaps it would be better to ignore
MI completely or adopt a wait-and-see attitude, because if it were to be
taken seriously and implemented, it might require a total transformation
of a number of business operations.

But in the 20-plus years since its first appearance, at least three major related developments have made it more difficult for professionals
committed to performance improvement to play ostrich. First, brain research has made major gains (Dennison and Dennison 1994; Carter
1998; Beeman and Bowden 2000). New professions have emerged, such
as cognitive psychologists, genetic physiologists, and cognitive programmers. The mapping of the learning pathways of the brain is offering
breakthroughs in many areas as extensive as those following the cracking of the genetic code. Indeed, the links between the two is shaping a
future research agenda of convergence. More relevant to this discussion, brain research not only has identified and confirmed the specific
pathways for each of the eight intelligences but also registered the electrical synergy of their interaction. In fact, Gardner's own initial research
began with examining brain-damaged patients and relating specific im-

pairments to intelligence deprivation. In short, the science of brain studies has served to anchor and to impart empirical credibility to MI's academic origins.

Second, Gardner himself has become less tentative and more aggressive and explicit about what MI is and has to offer (Gardner 1999). Largely emboldened by the successful educational applications of MI, he has argued that these various intelligences are not culturally or psychologically driven learning styles or preferences determined or shaped by history or fashion. Nor are they the precious monopoly of a small number of talented individuals or idiot savants who may be fortunate to be blessed or cursed with certain intelligences in abundance. Rather, they are congenitally the basic equipment of the human species. In fact, when Gardner was invited recently to give a speech on the occasion of 20 years since his book was first published, the subtitle of his address defined MI as "the optional taxonomy of human learning capacities" (2003). In short, MI is being presented as the new science of human potential. It has given new meaning and precision to Maslow's supreme goal of self-actualization.

Third, major changes in business training and performance improvement have taken place. The competitive quest to do more with less; to work smarter not harder; to raise levels of productivity, quality, customer satisfaction, and profitability and so forth have changed training, root and branch. Nonduplicative and cost-sensitive e-learning has come to the fore. The need for greater management and leadership of learning coupled with cost effectiveness led to the creation of corporate universities, learning management systems (LMS), and even new executives, CLO or CIO (chief learning/information officer) (Buchen 2002).

The net result is the recognition that attracting and retaining human capital requires constant upgrading. Training has in effect become a company's competitive edge. Yet because of the relentless pressure of the global economy not only to remain productive but also to exceed previous levels on the one hand, coupled with downsizing as perhaps the key American way of achieving such gains on the other hand, two disturbing future issues are emerging. Are there limits to productivity? Are there limits to learning? And are the two issues openly and/or secretly linked? In other words, asked again and again to repeat and even exceed the stretch goals of last year and perhaps in the process beginning to en-

counter the law of diminishing returns of productivity or its outer limits, CLOs, LMSs, and performance improvement professionals may be
more receptive to what MI has to offer. Fortunately, business does not
have to reinvent the wheel. The general and specific benefits MI can
provide already have been spelled out in 20 years of applications to education.

Limiting the focus to what business would value, two educational
patterns emerge. The first is disturbingly obvious: students graduating
from MI schools and curriculum gradually will apply to organizations
for jobs. Disparity will be immediately apparent, comparable perhaps
to students of e-learning coming to paper-and-pencil organizations. In
fact, almost all organizations are generally not aware of the extent to
which they are structured fundamentally to function as singular rather
than multiple intelligence organizations. In other words, these prospective new employees, many the best and the brightest, may compel a total review of basic organizational assumptions about intelligence. The
sign of a genuine challenge is that it affects both root and branch. Organizations may be forced to assess prospective candidates by Gardner's version of the key question: not "How smart are you?" but "How
are you smart?"

The second yield is more focused and may have a major impact on
recruitment and selection, promotion, team productivity, and ultimately training. Happily, the range of that change has already been
identified by educators. Below is a summary of the common operating
conclusions of different educators with varied curricula and at diverse
school levels on the value and application of MI to learning (for *teachers* read *trainers*, for *students, employees*) (Campbell, Campbell, and
Dickinson 1999).

MI teachers assume, develop expectations, and act on the belief that
students are intellectually competent in multifaceted ways. Students respond accordingly. The range of student responses and combinations of
intelligences are unlimited, elude final classification, and designate
long-term potential. The school's mission is rewritten to support and
promote intellectual diversity. Instructors become acute observers of
student learning behaviors, take their teaching cues from such observations, and link the immediate snapshot with the big picture, the short
term with the open ended.

Student learning is routinely multimodal. Teachers encourage and direct students to use their strong intelligences to work on and improve their weaker or less used intelligences. Students develop autonomous skills and habits through independent project learning. Self-reliance rules. Students develop collaborative and team skills and habits through multiage and differentiated groupings and through multidisciplinary and integrated studies. Interdependence rules. Finally, assessment takes as many multiple forms as there are intelligences, the favorites being rubric self-assessment, portfolios, simulations, and scenarios.

Although not all of the above impressive outcomes of education may carry over totally to business or performance, their principal value is compelling a review of what minimally would be required if MI were to be applied to business structures, operations, and human capital. Specifically, five reengineering principles can be distilled as guidelines for business:

1. *Inclusive*: Application to all employees at all levels at every stage of their development.
2. *Benchmark*: Initial identification is to be noted, factored, and followed by constant and seamless data tracking of potential.
3. *Alignment*: Individual employees and the company are joined at the hip; the process must be undertaken jointly and tested and monitored regularly by the degree of its reciprocity.
4. *Pervasive*: MI must permeate everything. Although ubiquitously invasive, initial foci on productivity and innovation, for example, may reflect company priorities.
5. *Interoperable*: MI also must define all work descriptions and interpersonal relationships to the point where in aggregated form they collectively become and sum up the company's mission.

Translating these guidelines into a plan requires a five-step process: identification, interpersonal dynamics, focus, reflection, and mission. The first stage is identifying the MI range of every employee. Happily, a number of assessment tools are available, all online (Accelerated Learning, BGRID, and Midas, for example). The more difficult task is replicating that process organizationally, which many companies have never undertaken. It requires defining what intelligences the organization values and predominantly uses. That is enriched by identifying the organization's preferred forms for communicating the range and diversity of its intelligences.

Sooner or later, such organizational self-assessment has to engage company vision and mission. If a task force of senior staff, middle-level managers, and representative employees were appointed to analyze and to tease out the essential intelligences assumed or implicit in those statements, and the input of human resources on the problem-solving and creative factors that actually have shaped hiring decisions and promotions were added, the final profile would identify the company's archetypal smarts and competitive edge. Whatever the results, the process of getting there would be enervating.

The next stage is contextually dynamic. The intelligences identified cannot remain as stills. They have to be animated in real time, terms, and work contexts. They have to appear as interactive and communicating behaviors operating in the environment and culture of the company. In other words, they have to be intrapersonal and interpersonal. Inevitably, this again involves a double assessment: how employees work together intelligently, and whether smart work flow and design as well as team performance are facilitated or impeded by company structures. The goal is to achieve optimum interoperability of smart interpersonal relationships and fluid environments.

The third stage follows Gardner's definition of the tasks of the eight intelligences in the first place. They all are involved in problem solving, creating innovation, and fulfilling goals (Gardner 1983, 1999). Of the three, the last is the mobilizer. To work effectively, MI needs goals and direction. MI is not self-activating or directing. It is driven by work or play. It reaches optimum levels when the two are fused. In education they are the learning goals of the school and the social goals of the community. In business they are the performance goals of productivity, quality, profitability, and customer service on the one hand, and the collective power of company vision and mission statements on the other. In other words, goals animate and direct MI, not the other way around. The companion task of the company then is integration: to determine the extent to which, by informed hiring and training, employees have the smarts to achieve smart goals.

The fourth stage may be the most difficult because it is the most individualistic, speculative, and fluid. It requires reflection and self-observation. Essentially, each employee has to generate a series of mininarratives or films that describe the interactive dynamics of their individual intelligences. The initial step only identified the intelligence inventory and range. Now that needs to be rendered interactively: why different intelligences organize themselves internally for problem solving and creativity. For example, one standard cluster typically may show one intelligence dominating and others in supportive role. In some other instances, a number are all equally and simultaneously active and contributing. But again, such self-assessment is not freewheeling but targeted by and against specific and recurrent work goals, activities, and patterns. What also needs to be emphasized is that this, like the first one of identification, is a benchmarking process. It establishes the growth point for each employee's future potential and thus sets the stage for a series of later growth steps.

The final stage of applications is where MI displays the full range of its potential applications. Minimally, what appear are critical applications to training, personnel, performance, and mission. In addition, the entire training menu and its delivery systems can be reviewed toward the end of being reshaped as a MI training program. In fact, the principal responsibility for implementing the five-stage MI process probably belongs to CLOs and directors of performance improvement and LMSs.

All personnel processes and procedures need to incorporate MI screening and assessment as conditions and criteria for initial hiring and subsequent promotion. But such a commitment to a new fusion of human capital and human potential in turn requires executive willingness to revisit and reformulate company vision and mission. In many ways and in the final analysis, the company unexpectedly is asked to play a larger and more proactive role through MI than through current modes of operation and measurement. MI also may grant organizations caught in ever-increasing spirals of having to outdo themselves with new way of doing so. Above all, it would provide business with the opportunity to display a vision and mission of embracing human potential rather than its dispensability.

Below is a visual summary of the five-step MI process:

MI APPLICATION STAGES

Process	Focus	Yields/Gains
1. Identification		
By individual	How are you smart?	Employee MI profile
By company	What do we value as smart?	Company MI profile
2. Interpersonal Assessment		
By individual	How are smarts interoperable?	Team smarts
By company	How does structure facilitate relationships?	Fluid design
3. Goals Focus: Customer		
By individual	Customer knowledge base?	Customer targets
By company	Knowledge gathering	Customer is data
4. Reflection		
A. By individual	How do smarts internally interact?	Synergy range
By company	What kind of interaction do we need?	Preferential patterns
B. By individual	How do team smarts interact?	Team optimums
By company	Structure to facilitate team work	Collaborative culture
5. HR Applications		
A. To training		
By individual	Problem solving and innovation	MI taxonomy
By company	Big picture and long term	Diagnostically driven training
B. Personnel		
By individual	Recruitment and selection	MI screening
By company	Promotion by smarts	MI reward system
C. Mission		
Of individual	Customer and innovation focused	Employee managers
Of company	MI organization	Future-driven

Clearly, MI is not a panacea or magic bullet. It can't solve systemic failures or executive lapses. It is also not a template of one-size-fits-all.

Companies like MI itself will display multiple MI versions and visions. Above all, it is not a quick fix. It requires trainers, HR and performance improvement professionals, and company leaders to pause, to step back, and to contemplate total reengineering.

Happily, it can be done in stages. It also can accommodate company priorities. Only certain divisions or operations can be initially targeted. But as training and human resource professionals link forces through MI, what in effect will gradually occur over time is that companies will be given a future lease on organizational life, and employees on their unfinished human potential. That double gain or integration is what in fact MI has to offer: the fusion of company and individual smarts.

REFERENCES

Armstrong, T. 2000. *Multiple intelligences in the classroom.* 2nd ed. Alexandria, Va.: ASCD.

Beeman, M. J., and E. M. Bowden. 2000. The right hemisphere. *Memory and Cognition.* 28, no. 7: 1,231–41.

Buchen, Irving. 2002. Directive and nondirective employees. *PI* 44, no. 2 (May).

Campbell, L., B. Campbell, and D. Dickinson. 1999. *Multiple intelligences and student achievement.* Alexandria, Va.: ASCD.

Carter, R. 1998. *Mapping the mind.* Berkeley: University of California Press.

Dennison, P., and G. Dennison. 1994. *Brain gym.* Ventura, Calif.: Edu-Kinestics.

Fogarty, R., and J. Stoehr. 1995. *Integrating curricula with multiple intelligences.* Palatine, Ill.: Skylight.

Gardner, Howard. 1983. *Frames of mind: The theory of multiple intelligences.* New York: Basic Books.

———. 1999. *Intelligence reframed: Multiple intelligences for the 21st century.* New York: Basic Books.

———. 2003. *Multiple intelligences after twenty years.* Paper presented at the meeting of the Educational Research Association on April 21.

Lazear, David G. 2001. *Multiple intelligence approaches to assessment.* Palatine, Ill.: Skylight.

Martin, J. 2001. *Profiting from multiple intelligences in the workplace.* Burlington, Vt.: Gower.

Martin, W. C. 1995. *Assessing multiple intelligences*. Paper presented at the International Conference on Educational Assessment in Ponce, PR, in March (ED 385 368).

Riggio, Ronald E., Susan E. Murphy, and Francis J. Pirozzolo, eds. 2002. *Multiple intelligences and leadership* (Kravis-de Roulet Leadership Conference). Mahwah, N.J.: Lawrence Erlbaum.

INNOVATION

26

INNOVATION RITES OF PASSAGE

The innovation industry has gone through three major phases. The first approach was represented by all the de Bonos—extremely bright, occasionally mystical advocates of creativity. Their writings spawned an incredible number of workshops. Organizations rapidly began to offer seminars full of wonderful activities. Everyone who attended enjoyed immensely the exotic exercises, but nothing or very little happened when they returned to their mundane jobs. No one was troubled by that evaluation because the expectations were minimal. If a few were affected, that was worth the investment. The intended gains were not urgently needed. And, of course, the entire effort contributed a new "paradigm" to everyone's vocabulary—creating or thinking outside the box.

Implicit in the first phase was the assumption that not everyone is creative. In part, the purpose of the workshops was discovery, especially self-discovery. But the poor record of implementation plus the more egalitarian belief that there were indeed more creative people around led to the second phase. A number of individuals from different disciplines turned away from dealing with individuals and instead favored the approach of supportive environments. Thus, recently, Geoffrey Colvin (Selden and Colvin 2003, 2004) rightly put to rest the notion that financial incentives stir creativity. He then went on to give three additional bits of advice. First, don't punish innovation failure. Second, hire creative people in the first place. Third, provide a secure environment. Colvin (2003) quotes Nigel Nicholson of the London Business School: "We thrive best as creative people under a stable plan we can comprehend. Space, safety, and support"— these are the optimum conditions for stimulating creativity. Colvin clinches his point for supportive environments by noting that of the best 100 companies to work for listed by *Fortune*, 18 of them had a no-layoff policy and outperformed all the others. Finally, Mihaly Csikszentmihalyi in his book *Creativity* (1996, 2) comes down squarely on supportive environments: "It is easier to enhance creativity by changing conditions in the environment than by trying to make people think more creatively."

Of course, one of the problems with choosing nurture over nature is the anxiety of many organizations to achieve results, especially those who are persuaded that the key to productivity on the one hand and to intense external competition on the other hand is innovation. Creativity is perceived not incorrectly as a breakthrough process matched only by high performance management. In short, Colvin and others may not be totally successful in persuading organizations to eschew punishment and to create the kind of environment that fosters creativity. But what is a significant about this second phase is the general recognition that the commitment of the first phase in the form of creativity workshops neither works, justifies the training costs, nor compensates for excessive expectations of innovation.

The third phase avoids totally the question of whether everyone or only certain people are creative. In fact, it generally bypasses the issue of creativity altogether. This phase is led by Peter Senge and the multiple variations that have followed in the wake of his *The Fifth Discipline* (1990, 3). Now we have Higgins IQ (intelligence quotient) as part of the general effort to identify and benchmark organizational intelligence (4). Indeed, the advocates for the learning organization have been generally successful in persuading companies to recognize the value and contribution of intellectual capital and to consider it a critical resource. To be sure, the only problem is that the emphasis on intellect and on problem-solving learning has generally excluded creativity, although the recent description of activities at Senge's incubator lab at MIT suggests that creativity may have come in through the back door. Efficacious though this phase has been, one unfortunate consequence is to put learning and creativity at odds with each other; or, as Michael Michalko (1998, 5) has argued: "Creativity is not the same as intelligence. An individual can be far more creative than intelligent or far more intelligent than creative."

Yes and no. The distinction is telling and strikes a chord of familiarity. Most intellectuals will freely confess and sometimes lament their lack of creativity. And many creative types will openly admit that they are not analytical but essentially intuitive. And so the stereotype of separation is perpetuated. Actually, the "truth" of Michalko's distinction is probably more a matter of developmental imprints than of endemic talents. After all, no one ever argued that the right side of the brain, when preferred, would then gobble up the left or vice versa in order for dominance to be total. In addition, all of us know creative people who are intelligent and intellectual, and analytical people who are creative and spontaneous. In short, the distinction between the two is not serviceable. More important, it is old and fails to reflect at least five major current changes and future challenges.

The first and most obvious development is the recognition of intellectual and creative capital. Under the gentle and comprehensive pressure of becoming a learning organization, professionals can acquire a more self-conscious sense of their contributions to a total research and development (R&D) commitment. Ideally, they *become* R&D. Reintroducing learning for midcareer professionals who have been away from school for one or two decades often mirrors going back to the university to take an advanced degree. Suddenly they discover how dated their bibliographies are. It is a jump start on getting to know the present. A second major development is organizational. Many companies have been reengineered, restructured, reconfigured. When the motive, as it often has been, is downsizing, the resultant environments are frequently not happy ones. More is being asked of less. Many thus would find it odd and even questionable that, given the needs of companies to achieve productivity breakthroughs, we should preciously exclude analytical skills from making the same contributions as creativity. Organizations seek to orchestrate their personnel so that it is not dominated by brass or woodwinds. Their goal is to be inclusive not exclusive. They are not about to discount a significant portion of their workforce to honor a romantic preference. Third, many organizations compelled to change are now asking, "Change to what?" They may have become leaner and meaner but they are the same organization except smaller. That may have been sufficient for short-term solvency and positioning, but that may not be adequate for future survival, let alone growth. Yet when reconfiguration involves a commitment to also installing a learning organization, that constitutes a genuine companywide investment in the future of the company. In other words, the organization itself becomes an actor in the drama of discovery.

A fourth major development that impacts this debate is the increasing use of teams, many of which are intentionally varied. Organizations indeed have found that the mix can be both creative and intellectually stimulating. In addition, progressive piggybacking frequently occurs. One type brings the process and problem to a point where the other picks it up; the initial one then comes back into the game and pushes the learning or creative curve further; and so on. It is like a slightly uneven tag race in which there is an unequal interdependence. Even when the team consists all of one type, the facilitator sets up the situation so that it requires intellectuals to take on the perspectives and behaviors of creativity, and creative types the perspectives and behaviors of analysis. Actually, the increasing use of facilitators and consultants in this way is another example of the ways in which organizations play an interventionist role to leverage discovery. Fifth and finally, a number of professionals in HR are increasingly recognizing and beginning to design workshops to bring together thinking and creating. What has emerged so far is the discovery that the process of stirring either involves the same rites of passage. One need not serve a life sentence as an intellectual who is never creative or a creative person who is never analytical. Altering perspectives, behaviors, perceptions, and so forth provides the promise of moving to the other side, no matter how tangentially, tenuously, or tentatively.

If we pause at this point to establish where we have been and where we are now, that might be helpful to also identify where we have yet to go. The first key claim is that intellectuality and creativity are not inherently opposed to each other. Most homogenous groups of either involve the difference of sameness. That needs to be supplemented by admixture or the difference of difference. In short, the thrust here is to bring the two together, in part because they can be stirred into action by the same rites of passage. The second claim involves linkage. Organizational and individual changes have to be folded into each other. Structure and human resources have to interface and even interpenetrate. Leadership between the two has to be acknowledged as shared and/or rotational.

In short, the comprehensive process for tapping both intellectuality and creativity has to always take place in an organizational setting, which, by virtue of that inclusion, will image a new organizational culture. Third, to accommodate both intellectual and creative types and to involve the organization, the learning organization I propose would have to become an unlearning organization. All the warnings and correctives mentioned earlier still would apply to this new version of the learning organization. Thus, Colvin and colleagues are absolutely correct: the environment must not be punitive or excessively impatient. (One company I consulted with had a six-month deadline.) Nicholson's safety, space, and support are an excellent trinity. Indeed, only then will employees believe senior management's commitment to intellectual and creative capital. But careful attention has to be paid to how the unlearning organization is introduced and wired in place, just as care and focus must be involved in communicating decisions. Therefore, the fourth issue is the need to find a "mechanism" to implement the process. The way it is launched may determine its outcomes. There should be no fanfare— no cheerleading exhortations, no references to the new saviors of the company, no elaborate pompous policy statements. And, of course, no financial incentives or deadlines. A mechanism is neutral. It does not draw attention to itself. It requires no monitoring or recordkeeping. An excellent example was that used by 3M a number of years ago. One day it was announced that starting on Monday everyone would be allowed to spend 15 minutes each day on some idea or activity or invention that interested the employee. Prior approval was not required. There were no restrictions on what it could be. There was no timetable or deadline. The only limitation was that it could not exceed 15 minutes a day or a total of 75 minutes per week, and all regular assignments had to be completed.

The arrangement produced an environment that was quietly electric, like that of a research university or Bell Labs, except that 3M was more rapidly productive and less pompous. It worked like a charm. Innovation emerged, and from both types: the analytical problem solvers and the creative problem solvers. Clearly, a neutral mechanism is as good for the goose as for the gander. Above all, employees were generally happier and more involved in their regular work, and each one seemed to have a look of special glee as if he or she were going to be the 3M Edison.

The fifth factor is that the same stimuli, encouraging environments, and above all dislocations, work equally well with thinking and with creating. For both thinking and creativity to progress and deepen, they have to undo themselves. Incrementalism will not work. More thinking is not what is needed. Different thinking, even nonthinking or intuitive thinking, needs to be called forth. It is not more learning that is needed but more *un*learning. The same is true of creativity. It is not working outside the box but sometimes becoming the box and working one's way out. It is at this point where the organization also becomes a key player. That role is not limited to serving as a benevolent provider of a kinder, gentler environment or obediently providing training funds. Rather, the organization becomes a partner involved in the process of developing its potential. In many ways, it is the structural aggregate of the growth of its intellectual and creative professionals and their contributions. Indeed, in many ways their development becomes the future of the organization.

Finally, the goal of unlearning is futuristic. It is not enough to become smarter and to be current. Unlearning has to introduce the intellectuals and the creative types to the ways of the future. One does not approach or journey to the future in some chronological or sequential manner. It is not the traditional strategic planning process. The future happens when other things happen. It cannot be summoned or invoked. It cannot be commanded to be. It is oblique or tangential. It is initially out of focus. It responds only to the incantation and conjuring of intellectual, creative, and organizational discovery. In many ways, my argument here resembles that advanced in *Competing for the Future* (Hamel and Prahalad 1994), except that their discussion is about strategy and structure and not intellectuality and creativity (7). Their notion is that it is not enough merely to reengineer and hopefully in the process become more productive and profitable, welcome though those short-terms gains are; rather, one has to create something different, to reinvent even the industry. Access to the future, they rightly argue, is not facilitated by more of the same old stuff, no matter how it has been repackaged. In fact, chances are, if what the company comes up with does not resemble anything around it, it is probably the future. On an individual scale, my argument is that both intellectuality and creativity to achieve productivity gains require the same dislocation from the present and current way of thinking and envisioning. And here too, if the perspectives that emerge are sufficiently different, they also are the future. In other words, what I am proposing is that the organizational focus of Hamel and Prahalad be supplemented. If their description of organizational intervention were to be expanded to include the creation of an unlearning organization on the one hand, and to embrace the mutual and interactive development of both intellectuals and creative people alike on the other hand, the result would be a powerful triangulation. In addition, it would be now the enhanced role of the intellectual and the creative people to gradually transform the entire organization into a learning organization for the present and then into the future.

One final task: the common rites of passage that stir intellectual and creative people to more of what they are, to cross over and ultimately emerge in a different space and time. I have written elsewhere about the process of unlearning, but since then I have been involved in a number of training sessions to determine ways or approaches of encouraging unlearning and finding the future. What I would like to describe, no matter how tentatively, are some of the rites of passage that can be used to affect both groups and that to some extent also describe what the organization can be exposed to as well. This double convergence is probably the most important way the future happens.

For the future to be stumbled upon, dislocation is required. Strategic reconfigurations or individual displacements of talents do not happen automatically or without forethought. The trick is to plan the haphazard, and to discipline somewhat the dislocation, whether it is individualized, group, or organizationally orchestrated. There is no authoritative list of steps. There is no infallible sequence. What is needed is a suspension of success, a surrender of the status quo, a rejection of history. For organizations contemplating the creating of a new division apart from their core business, it is recommended that they set up that new venture as a separate business so that it requires a new way of thinking and performing unencumbered by the core past.

Another problem with setting up a list of the rites of passage is that lists are tyrannical and prescriptive, whereas the truth is that the rituals are a revolving door through which one can enter and leave at any point. What follows, therefore, is not meant to be a definitive and exhaustive series of all possibilities but an identification of the different trigger areas available to stir change. It is a list of raw materials that may all go into the finished product. Indeed, it is ultimately invitational. It serves as a series of new or enhancing containers that only each individual can fill.

All the factors listed below are behavioral or habitual. As such, they are paradoxical. They offer security but at a price of freedom. They offer "safety, space, and support" but often render beneficiaries inert. The discipline of dislocation thus involves some risk. As far as motivation is concerned, if one is a happy prisoner and not persuaded that one is stuck, then what will move employees to change? Only the desperation of failure or the heady intoxication of being born again—each leading compulsively to the other. The factors listed are like icons designed to be contemplated as part of a risk reassessment. As such, they are static and become animated only with the input of change and playfulness. Thus, the learning organization encourages these kinds of questions: "What if I were to do this differently . . .?" "What would things be like if I changed this way or that?" "What would things look like if we could start from scratch?" The unlearning organization turns the tables in the questioner and pries control away from that central "I" that positions itself always in the driver's seat. Thus, other questions emerge: "How would this problem go about solving itself?" "What would be the version of this problem or situation in 2020?" "How would God solve this problem?"

VARIABLE CONDITIONS OF DISCIPLINED DISLOCATION

1. Distance

Familiarity may or may not breed contempt, but it certainly locks in behavior. Many love their habits, whether it is the morning get-up system or packing a bag for travel. So how does one create the difference of distance? IBM abandoned many of their plush, mostly unused, offices for "warehouse" facilities that agents visited when needed. Although it had all the basics, it was not a permanent resting place and required a kind of flexibility not called for in traditional settings. To think or create differently, perspective has to change. One cannot be in the same place and at the same distance from work and problems. Distance changes the angle of vision, even the overall shape of the object. Up close or very far, it magnifies or eliminates background. Change distance, and one can change thinking and creating.

2. Time

This is the other axis of distance. The schedule runs the scheduler. The major complaint one hears from managers is insufficient time. The focus here, however, is not finding more time but finding more different time, like 3M, and doing things at times that are at variance with habit—getting up earlier or later, wasting time, coming late for an appointment and developing a creative excuse, and so on. The key is to make time your ally, not your enemy—to use it to become your partner in crime and creativity.

3. Space

Most occupy and even cherish the same spaces again and again. The same chair, the same favorite pen, scissors; above all, the same work space. We snuggle in and say "Ahhh." But as Robert Frost pointed out poetically: "Before I built a wall I'd ask to know/What I was walling in or walling out." The illusion of choice: Have we chosen the space, or has the space chosen us? Are we grooved to be and think and work in certain ways because of the force of outer space? Does our outer space affect our inner space? Do all externals affect internals? What would be the reverse effect? The inward becomes the outward.

4. Order

Aristotle advised artists to begin *media res*—in the middle of things—in order to create the drama of unfolding. Intellectuals, especially linear sequential types, always start with the beginnings of things. Square one has its structural equivalent in organizations that follow the order of top-down or chain of command. The vertical and the horizontal are ultimately identical. An organization structured according to Margaret Wheatley's (Wheatley and Kellner-Rogers 1996) river that flows through it or Tachi Kiuchi's (1997) incredible diversity of a rain forest would be closer to the Aristotelian ideal. So order becomes another one of those paradoxical trade-offs—the desk without anything on it except a pen, and the one overflowing with papers, books, folders, and underneath a half-eaten sandwich. Could there ever be a crossover? That would be the way of madness or change.

5. Initiative

Charles Handy (2002) invoked the wonderful image of the doughnut to explain much about organizations and the way they operate
(9). Of course it is an English, not an American, doughnut. Where
the American doughnut has a hole, the English has jelly. There is the
core and the space that surrounds it. The core is what one *has to* do,
while the surrounding space is what one *can* do. There are many individuals and organizations that are core-obsessed. Freedom is kept
to a minimum. In that case, notes Handy, the core becomes a chore.
Its accomplishment is a necessary evil, sometimes more evil than
necessary. The most lamentable dimension of all this is the employee
who forsakes or converts the outer space into the core or the organization that encourages that kind of limiting self-absorption. What
that does is sentence the organization and the individuals it is com-
posed of to a life sentence of repetition. In one company I worked
with, we gave a test group a new ID—Initiative Diaries. That was our
mechanism to lure them into outer space. And it worked. For higher-
order intellectuals and artists, they also might benefit by reading
chaos theory.

6. Complicate and Simplify

"To enjoy something, you need to increase its complexity. As Herodo-
tus remarked, 'We cannot step in the same river twice'" (Csikszentmihalyi 1996, 350). Often we stop too soon. We live too short and die too
long—we settle for an answer and then stay with its success forever.
Thus, ironically, premature success can seal us off from the difference of
the future. Complexity can occur by seeking root causes. The Japanese
recommend that for any problem, "why" needs to be asked at least five
times. But complexity is neither an end in itself nor endless. Complexity
will signal that its depth has been tapped when what emerges is essentially simple, basic, and recurrent.

7. Seek Opposites

There is a need to violate your Myers-Briggs profile. John Gardner
was essentially an introvert but, to accomplish many of his goals he had
to be involved politically as a lobbyist and become a fund-raiser. He had

to become what internally he was not, yet his vision propelled him. Everyone lives with his or her opposite. It is difficult for competitive people to become cooperative, however that happens regularly in team dynamics. The problem is that we characteristically deepen our grooves. We go to the same conferences with the same kinds of people. We listen to the same kind of music, read the same books and magazines, and talk the same way to the same people. And then we wonder why we are bored or stale. The reason organizations have to become more proactive and even aggressive is that, left to one's private inclinations, opposites will not be embraced. Organizations calculatingly need to introduce new rites of passage and change habits and behaviors. That is what the creation of supportive environments and training are really all about.

8. Indulgence

Most purists are puritanical. They cannot abide dilution or admixture, and to do so is to appear self-indulgent. But another way to look at it is to regard it as playful. Intellectuals need to appreciate essays, and creative types, mathematics. A critical antidote is science fiction, which Asimov (1980) rightly defined as an escape to reality. The best of science fiction is a fusion of the intellectual and the creative. To admire the genre is in effect to embrace that model of fusion. What a future-driven organization needs to become is a work of science fiction. The indulgence an organization has to sanction is a variation of Asimov's definition.

9. Generational Exposure

Consort with new hires. A smart organization will facilitate that happening. Potentially, they are from another time and planet. Conversations with this different generation will bring about the same dislocation as confronting the future. But for that to happen and for receptivity to be total, offer no wisdom unless it is calculated to stir reactions that are different. To heighten the entire experience, take full advantage of whatever diversity there is among the new.

10. Identify a Retirement Career

Cultivate the illusion of a later difference—of doing something later when all the momentum of sameness has been exhausted and we have paid our dues many times over. It is amazing how creative professionals are about living a life that they have never led. Hardly any organization compels that kind of thinking or preparation for it, although it is a wonderfully proactive way of engaging the future in the present. The notion of actually engaging and preparing for that later prospect is itself an intellectually and creative way of becoming someone else and thinking differently. And in this case, this is no mere exercise but a real-life occasion for making the future happen.

In summary, then, if organizations seek to have the future happen for them and their employees, they need to do the following. First, they need to combine, not separate, intellectuality and creativity. Second, if they have put in place learning organizations they need to go to the next phase and make them unlearning organizations so as to move beyond incrementalism. Third, they need to assume a proactive and interventionist role as a facilitator of difference. Fourth, they need to create supportive environments and find mechanisms to enhance and deliver difference. Fifth, they need finally to identify and support the rites of passage both for individuals and the company so that they move together toward discovery and reinvention. When an organization and its people unlearn enough to become science fiction, then the future happens.

REFERENCES

Asimov, Isaac. 1980. Editorial: Escape to reality. *Isaac Asimov's Science Fiction Anthology* 3 (Spring–Summer).

Csikszentmihalyi, Mihaly. 1996. *Creativity: Flow and the psychology of discovery and invention.* New York: HarperCollins.

Frost, Robert. 1969. *The Poetry of Robert Frost: The Complete Poems, Complete and Unabridged.* Edited by Edward C. Latham. New York: Henry Holt.

Hamel, Gary, and C. K. Prahalad. 1994. *Competing for the future.* Boston, Mass.: Harvard Business School Press.

Handy, Charles. 2002. *The elephant and the flea: Reflections of a reluctant capitalist.* Boston, Mass.: Harvard Business School Press.

Kiuchi, Tachi. 1997. *Lessons from the rain forest.* Paper presented at the annual meeting of the World Future Society, San Francisco.

Michalko, Michael. 1998. *Cracking creativity: The secrets of creative genius.* Berkeley, Calif.: Ten Speed Press.

Selden, Larry, and Geoffrey Colvin. 2004. *Killer customers: Tell the good from the bad and crush your competitors.* New York: Portfolio/Penguin.

———. 2003. *Angel customers and demon customers: Discover which is which and turbo-charge your stock.* New York: Portfolio.

Senge, Peter M. 1990. *The fifth discipline: The art and practice of the learning organization.* New York: Doubleday/Currency.

Wheatley, Margaret, and Myron Kellner-Rogers. 1996. Self-organization, strategy and leadership. *Strategy and Leadership* (Strategic Leadership Forum) 24 (July–August): 18–24.

27

CREATIVE THRESHOLDS

Preparing the way for creating anything new is a neglected art. It requires anticipatory reflection and creative thresholds instead of direct and impatient assault. A case example: The senior management of a small high-tech firm made an executive decision to promote company-wide innovation. That was summarily announced not only as a crash course but also a crusade. Everyone in the organization would be involved. A designated steering group was appointed. Tangible results were to emerge within six months. Breakthroughs would be rewarded with one-time bonuses.

Does all of the above sound disturbingly familiar? Does any of it cause you to squirm and groan? Or do you find nothing wrong? In any event, by the time six months came around, the company had nothing to show for its efforts. As a consequence, three of its vice presidents (marketing, human resources, and strategic planning) were dismissed. Then, troubled and confused, the CEO decided to call in a consultant with the idea of performing a quick fix and cleaning up the debris. I was that consultant.

Our first meeting started off with the CEO venting for ten minutes. My reaction was to listen and to wait patiently and then afterward to slow everything down and try to engage him in a general if not almost philosophical discussion of innovation. "Innovation is one of the most difficult objectives to accomplish. It is never easy to introduce. Its definition is slippery. Many argue as to what's really innovative and what isn't. And whether everyone is creative."

Then I moved on to specifics. "How many of your managers in your judgment exhibit innovation? What percentage of the workforce do you estimate are creative? Do you believe employees can be trained to be creative, or is such ability basically innate?" We also talked about innovations that occurred in the past in the company, as well as in the industry. What were they? Who brought them forth?

My strategy was to suggest that innovation is complex and not in the same league as announcing a salary increase or benefit package. In short, my goal was to encourage a more reflective and deliberative approach. I tried to give the impression that we both had all the time of the world to sort this thing out.

The approach worked. In closing the session, I suggested we meet again the next day to go over what apparently hadn't work and why that was the case. The CEO responded: "Let's make it early in the day before things get cluttered and my time is gobbled up."

I found the CEO the next morning, not anxious to have another philosophical discussion but instead eager to get down to cases. His game plan clearly was to come up with a new and this time successful launching process for innovation in the company. I was reluctant to totally abandon the process of dialogue or lose what had been captured the day before. But the CEO was hot to trot, so I tried to weave together all three elements of reflection, evaluation, and action—what I viewed as the essential trinity for preparing the way for all new initiatives.

"OK, "I said, "but first let's look at how we launched this initiative in the first place." That immediately puzzled the CEO. "Why should an announcement even be an issue for reflection, evaluation, and action?"

"We could get into an extensive discussion of how you announce decisions in general," I responded. "But I know you are anxious to get to the heart of this particular situation. So let me just ask whether there is anything special about innovation—the way that we talked about it yesterday—that might affect the way the announcement was made?"

The CEO, musing out loud, recalled, "Many are uneasy about innovation; many feel they are not creative. And I would even say that many may not know what innovation is, or be fully aware of what it could mean to the future of this company."

"Exactly! Given all these apparently legitimate concerns and hidden questions," I asked, "what, in retrospect, would you have done differently about announcing the initiative?"

"With the benefit of hindsight, I guess I would have discussed it first. I would have used examples. Big ones, and many little ones, as many I could think of; some of those we talked about yesterday. I might have told them the story of what was done at 3M. You know, that article you gave me on their 15-minute system. . . . Above all, I would try to strike a balance. While I don't want innovation to appear facile or accidental, I also don't want it to appear distant and impossible, beyond their reach, reserved for only R&D types."

"Good! So now we know that we can't just drop an announcement like a bomb without taking the chance that it will blow up in our face. OK, so that was not the best way to start, and you already have to found another way. It is interesting that you mentioned R&D. A little sidebar if I might."

The CEO nodded and leaned forward. I continued, "Thomas Edison still holds the record for more patents than anyone else to this day. Of course, he may have been an inventing genius, but he had others working with him who were not Edisons. So he developed for himself and all his employees idea quotas. But he also knew that some ideas were big and that many would be small; so, for example, he gave himself six months to come up with one new major idea and a number of smaller ones. I mention Edison because he may be telling us something. His emphasis was not on inventions but ideas. Maybe that holds a key for the company and innovation. Maybe the process we want to get going is IG—Idea Generation. And maybe what we have to do is to encourage each employee to work on his ID—his own Idea/Innovation Diary—which is private and not available to anyone unless the employee says it is."

The CEO nodded reflectively. "You're right. The focus is really on ideas. We can't all be Edisons and match his record, but if we can get our people to write down what they think and what they have come up with, we will be way ahead of the game. In fact, I never told anyone this, but I keep an idea journal by my bedside. OK, let's keep going. This is good stuff."

"Let's go on to the next point. The initiative was presented as a crash course and a crusade. Put yourself in your employees' place. How would you have reacted to such a statement?"

The CEO snapped, "I would have resented it. I don't like being stampeded into anything. And I personally don't warm to the cheerleader role. Worst of all, it sets us up for success or failure. We either make it, or we fold. Besides, nothing could be further from the truth. We are actually doing quite well, and all indications are that we will have solid sales for the next three to five years. So this was a future-oriented activity. But, OK, I see where you are going. What you are saying is that we should have just told it like it really is—as way of getting a leg up, ensuring our future success. Right?"

"Absolutely," I quickly answered. "And maybe even to grow another business or at least another division. When the juices start to flow, you never finally know what people will come up with. Now, pressing on, why a timetable of six months?"

The CEO bristled, "Now I think that was perfectly defensible. You can't have an open-ended arrangement without limits and without closure. I would let that stand."

"OK," I said and then paused, "but suppose nothing happens within 6 months. Do you shut everything down or let it just go on? Or suppose then something surfaces by month 7, something else by month 8. What then? How will that 6-month deadline look?"

The CEO interrupted: "Maybe arbitrary, even dumb. But there has to be some oversight and control. They have to know that they will be held accountable."

I mildly protested, "But accountable for what? You did not put a dime into this. You are not providing any training. You are not giving people time off. You are not sending them to any conferences. You are not even buying them books and magazines to read. You put this pot of money aside for bonuses, but if no one comes up with anything even that money won't be spent. I understand every executive's need for control and outcomes, but deadlines and innovation are not compatible, unless you are willing to settle for half-baked goods prematurely delivered before their time."

The CEO was quiet. Had I pushed too hard? I stepped back and took another tack. "Instead of control, you may want to go for indirect monitoring. Schedule weekly brown bag or pizza lunches (you pay). Mix divisions, levels, shifts. Have the supervisors just listen; tell them not to talk, just take notes. Carry forward those notes to the next level, then to the next, and then to senior management. Walk around, drop in on sessions unexpectedly, listen for a change."

The CEO sighed, "Well, it makes sense not to dictate creativity. It's like pushing spaghetti—it just won't behave the way you want it to. Well I guess you're also questioning my picking an innovation steering group. Did I do anything right?"

I said reassuringly, "You came up with idea of an innovation initiative, and that is right as rain. But I am curious. What was your thinking here? What did you hope to accomplish with this steering committee?"

The CEO sat back and thought. "Well, we picked people from each division. Each had an excellent record and had given some evidence of being creative. The idea was they would model for each of their divisions the behaviors to produce results."

I agreed. "That makes a lot of sense. Modeling is critical. That is what Edison did. But here's my problem. It's either going to be companywide or it is not. It is either going to be collective or not. Innovation often occurs with the least likely people and in the least likely ways. Besides, most selected steering groups are political. Those chosen are always the same ones picked. The winners of trips to Hawaii are always the ones who win again and again. Good for the few winners, lousy for all the rest who may get used to being losers; and there are always more losers than winners. Besides, everyone in the division will rib their representative to death and make him regret they ever were chosen in the first place. Finally it will be seen as a transparent way again of maintaining control. Make it egalitarian. Inclusive not exclusive. Fish or cut bait."

The CEO protested, "OK, OK, but what's wrong with incentives? It's been used since the beginning of time and it works."

I conceded, "You're right. Generally it works. It certainly has been effective for years—in sales especially. But money and innovation have nothing to do with each other. It is a mismatch. Incentives stimulate only the familiar, not the different. Besides, such incentive-driven innovations will generate a lot of look-alikes of what you already have. But you will not get anything different."

The CEO was not ready to toss in the towel, "Well, what should we do? Drop the idea of incentives altogether?"

I again became reflective. "I am not sure. My instinct tells me that it is a question the employees should tackle. See what they come up with. Make it part of the creative challenge. I have to confess, I am a little old-fashioned. To me the best incentive is the future of the company—the future of my job. Or as one worker put it to the COO, 'Your job is to keep this company around so that I can collect my pension.'"

The CEO leaned forward. "I agree. I am old-fashioned that way too. And that worker is right. You can't have growth and change unless you are around to try both. But it's the executive's job to look ahead and to decide now what will keep us around later."

He stood up and held out his hand. "Well, I think our exchange has set us on a new course. I now see why care must be taken with certain initiatives—preparing the way as you call it—thinking it through. I would like you to stay with us on this project, through all the stages for as long as it takes."

"Be happy to do so."

"And let's get together soon and hold another seminar. OK, professor?"

Postscript: I nodded smiling and said to myself, "He was right on both counts. I am a professor and it was a seminar." But after I left and was walking down the hall, I realized that he was a professor as well, and that good seminars are always shared if they are to be seminal.

In any case, in less than three months, three major employee-generated proposals for innovation passed the review committee and were on their way to implementation. Many others followed. All were energized by the idea/innovation diary, which often led to small nondramatic changes that could not be called innovative but just different ways of doing things. Above all, the employees entrusted with the future of their jobs and the company rose to the challenge and became preeminent and permanent idea-generators.

In the process, what were the lessons learned? Innovation should never just be announced. Preparation is required. Examples should be given from the company itself, from the industry. Innovation should not appear facile or fortuitous but never beyond reach of the rank and file. Speed is not relevant. Deadlines are the enemy of creativity. If you have to have quotas, stress a number of ideas. Urge all to develop an idea/innovation diary. Deadlines and innovation are not good partners. Keep all open ended, like the process itself. But stir the pot. Schedule weekly brown bag lunches. Top management should not pick innovation teams. The effort is either collective or it is not. Besides, it is not a political popularity contest. Money and innovation have nothing to do with each other. That is a crass mismatch and will stimulate not difference but incremental familiarity. If you need an incentive system, let it be employee designed. It is likely to be creative in its own right.

The ultimate preconditions for innovation are environmental. The key variables are identified and summarized below:

Situation	From	To
1. Culture	Directive	Questioning
2. Focus	Same	Different
3. Structure	Closed	Open
4. Systems	Mechanical	Biological
5. Information	Limited	Shared
6. Distribution	Insiders	Network
7. Communication	Vertical	Horizontal
8. Status	Official	Unofficial
9. Incentives	Financial	Environmental
10. Quality	Prescribed	Evolving

28

RADICAL BREAKTHROUGHS

Desperation sometimes leads to radical creativity. For example, imagine creating a change pill. With one stroke, workers would change; so would teams, so would managers, so would organizations. To many frustrated CEOs and consultants, it seems that this is what it would take. So much already has been done, written, and researched about changing or reengineering people and organizations, and so much has been tried with often unimpressive or short-term results, that we seem to be at the end of our rope. Perhaps we have finally reached the point where we can contemplate going off the deep end—pursuing desperation rather than enlightenment, considering excesses rather than rational incentives.

The basic reason change is difficult is that people are stuck in success. The tried, the true, and the tested have generally served them well. Their basic problem-solving toolkit has worked most or all of the time. The kinds of benevolent and often heady learning dislocations that occurred in college or graduate school have been replaced by steady and sober affirmations of standardized operations and hard-nosed conventional wisdom. In many cases, work development has been continuous rather than discontinuous, incremental rather than different.

In short, whom are we asking to change? Someone who has been successfully set in his ways, who already is persuaded he has been changing and growing for many years, who has acquired the language and behaviors of change via various workshops and books, and who has learned to pick the fruits of productivity from the lowest branches.

Also many current efforts to change behaviors and environments are manipulative, punitive, or excessive. Workers are offered rewards or gain-sharing incentives. Employing a more direct frontal attack, employees are told that if they fail to achieve their stretch goals, the company will find others who will. Finally, CEOs and managers communicate endlessly: they talk about global competition, industry problems, customer alienation, and many similar topics. But it mostly falls on deaf ears because what all these techniques translate into is a request or demand to do more. What is needed is not more of the same stuff but different stuff—innovative stuff.

In a nutshell, what are we seeking to accomplish, and how far are we willing to go? If the goals are basically incremental, then we will get more of the same; and if that is acceptable, then stay with the manipulative, punitive, and excessive.

But if the goal is something more substantial and radical—to change the fundamental assumptions and perspectives of inquiry, thinking, and conceptualization—then we have to engage in a strategy that is more oblique and even mischievous. In the process we have to outflank success. We have to come from the side and from the back and from the top and the bottom. We have to unthink our basic way of thinking. We have to unlearn our basic way of learning. We have to unlive our basic way of living. We have to become, in short, someone different. The enemy is thus not outside but inside the gates. The strategy being proposed here is threefold.

Instead of asking for change, ask for innovation. It does not make any sense to beat around the bush. Go for the brass ring. Whether or not you are officially a learning organization, if you become an innovative one you will be an outstanding learning organization—for innovation is the ultimate learning experience.

Recognize that the brain is designed for survival. It becomes creative only when survival is imperiled—in other words, dislocation drives openness. Outflanking the brain and its successful habits is initially slow. The mind has to be weaned gradually; it has to be teased into being surprised by itself. But once a new flow starts, movement can be rapid.

What follows below is a series of dislocations designed to gradually separate the familiar from the different. In increasing intensities, the aim is to move the center off center in order to create the space for the gradual emergence of a new center. This new center may not be really totally new. It may be a previous center in which the experience of creativity occurred and in which learning was still incomplete.

The goal is to bring that past forward into the present, not to compete or replace the present identity but to complement and converse with it. The ultimate synthesis will be a fusion of the old and the new. It introduces a new tension between success and exploration, between the operating reality of the tried and the true and the experimental and the new.

The first strategy involves a gentle disorientation produced by assumptions analysis. That helps to set up an other-than linear or either-or kind of thinking. The second invites the dislocation of adopting a totally new temporariness, of looking at the world and problems as transitional, always unfinished. The third and last is the most destructive and vigorous because it involves a process of emptying the self and the mind, casting out the obstacles remaining to a new curiosity and experimentation.

I. DISORIENTATION OF ASSUMPTIONS

The first step of exploring assumptions involves, in this case, innovation itself. Here are five pairs of statements:

1. Innovation is easy.
   Innovation is hard.
2. Creativity is something you are born with.
   Creativity is something you acquire.
3. Everyone is creative.
   Only a few are creative.
4. Intellect inhibits creativity.
   Intellect supports creativity.
5. Creative types are strange.
   Creative types are normal.

Typically, individuals choose one half of each pair. And usually a divide is set up between analysis and innovation, with each group following a consistent pattern of self-identification. Thus, those who are highly intellectual often construct the following composite:

"Innovation is hard except for those who are born with it. These few creative types are often anti-intellectual and eccentric."

The other construction is 180 degrees away:

"Innovation is relatively easy, especially for those who are used to it, although one learns all the time. Creative people think but not primarily; and they are not so much weird as different, sometimes."

So there we are, each group passing a half off as a whole. In addition, a number of permanent and false oppositions are proclaimed: innate versus acquired, intellect versus creativity, normal versus abnormal, easy versus hard. The first conclusion one therefore can come to is that such divisiveness is the sign of being stuck on one side or other of the brain. The process of constantly confirming that precious partiality is the very antithesis of innovation. The proper answer to all five pairs is duality: not one or the other but both. Innovation is both easy and hard, born with and acquired, resistant and accepting of intellect, strange and normal, and available to all but especially to a few. In short, the first stage of change is to establish harmonious discord, dwelling comfortably and without irritation with opposites, and becoming comfortable with ambiguity.

2. THE INCOMPLETION OF TRANSITION

Creative dislocation needs to be followed by another disorientation: an introduction to precarious states of mercurial thinking and imagining. Enter the five terrible T's: the temporary, the tenuous, the transitional, the transient, and the tentative. The aim of any one or all five of these icons is to breed impermanence, to create a willing suspension of disbelief that anything will last or be unique. It is an acceptance of footsteps in the sand, a recognition that what will emerge or be produced will not dominate the landscape forever. The Etruscans painted on wood knowing full well—unlike their Roman counterparts—that it would eventually crumble, just the way they would.

To flourish, innovation requires a sense of experimentation—it cannot be oppressed by permanence and its companion fear of making mistakes. The forms must be made of rubber, not concrete. Nothing must be etched in stone. Edifices first exist as scaffolding. Drafts must become the norm. A Tinkertoy mentality shall reign supreme. Things should be put together and taken apart again and again, not desperately or with anxiety, but with a sense of play and even mischief.

The new attitude to be gradually developed is that there is no end to anything or any activity. There is no final solution to any problem. Rather, the best is temporary—it is what we currently can create. But nothing is finished, and the evolution of the organization is far from over. It may have future incarnations that are not known or anticipated. The current products and services provided may not be what will be offered or created five or ten years from now. The company may become more of an electronic than an actual place. And most important it will say: "I am not finished—I am not done with myself yet."

The net result is that everything is shaken out and loosened up. Everything becomes subject to flow rather than molded into a divisionalized or standardized finality. Rather than only and always being masters of our fate and captains of our ships, we become objects as well as subjects of that flow. Work becomes more interesting. We are carried along. We are not totally known or owned. There is a permanent transience to all things, an unfinished and incomplete series of expectations that workers are invited to compete and finish, no matter how tenuously.

Once this kind of thinking takes hold, employees become multidimensional rather than singularly focused on the one way to do things. Curiously, then, transition becomes not only a new norm but also a new source of difference.

3. EMPTYING OUT THE VESSEL

The last strategy is made easier by the first two. At this point, the world and the employee experiences a sense of multiple impressions. There is déjà vu as previous experiences of creativity and learning are tapped again. There is a dawning and growing respect for complexity and ambiguity—that things are not what they seem, that there are links and connections not previously acknowledged, that the world is more entangled and perhaps more secretly and subtly interconnected than initially appeared. And, finally, the knowledge that every current way of doing or conceiving of things masks many alternatives that were not chosen and many others that were not originally thought of. The rush to get on with things is tempered by the recognition of constant change and transience. Above all, there is the sense that there is more to everything, especially me, and there is enough time to do all the things worth doing.

At this last stage, the individual turns on himself all the altered states that he (or she) has experienced in order to claim himself anew and to make himself whole and wholly his own. This is the most reflective stage. It involves a double process of emptying oneself and being filled up. The worker must trash his mind and purge it of everything but the problem he is trying to solve. His world must be occupied by that problem. There is no past or future, only the present. Rather than irritably being busy with his problem-solving toolkit, he has to go quiet so that he can hear what the problem has to say to him, including its solution or, more accurately, its solutions. And when that happens, change occurs, innovation appears, and the future is incarnated.

Risky strategies? Perhaps. But the gains are potentially great. Besides, the only way organizations will be able to claim their future is if they grant it fully to their employees first.

29

INNOVATION TRAINING

Remember Robert Frost's classic warning for those involved in boundary-setting and measurement? "Before I built a wall I'd ask to know/ What I was walling in or walling out." Frost must have had creativity in mind, because assessing innovation is comparable to performing an autopsy on a living subject.

Innovation is always more busy than still, more a motion picture than a series of snapshots. Process trumps product; the journey is always superior to arrival; Know-Why ultimately drives Know-How. The genius of the Deming–Japanese partnership was not quality—that was only its defining sign—but innovation. The achievement was an unwavering commitment not solely to continuous improvement but continuous innovation.

Everything was grist for the mill, especially the obvious. And worker comfort and intelligence were as much objects for improvement as quality-driven products and services. In short, to ensure that quality was not an add-on applied at the end of the assembly line, innovation was distributed, embedded, and practiced throughout the entire process. Indeed, innovation became the overarching process itself.

The obvious solution of copying the Japanese, which many have tried, has generally failed. The reasons for the lack of easy transference, however, are instructive, for they also define the three major obstacles and issues confronting all innovation training:

1. *Organizational*. A commitment to innovation cannot be superficial or partial. Rather, it compels a total change in company culture, mission, and structure. Specifically, it requires the creation of an environment receptive to the discontinuity of creativity.
2. *Training*. Can creativity even be taught? Or is it like leadership, inborn not acquired? Then too, how does it fit in with current program array? Does it displace the current focus on productivity? The relationship between innovation and all other training is part and parcel of working out the larger relationship between innovation and productivity.
3. *Workforce and Management*. What is the innovation capacity of employees? Should creativity training be available across the board? With what costs? And what about generating expectations that may be disappointed?

Although the emphasis here is on the last point, innovation training, if it is not to be stillborn, ultimately requires bringing together and converging the other two dimensions of the challenge. Indeed, much of the formidable nature of developing innovation training derives from its obvious and hidden entanglements with organizational structures and training capacity.

An examination of post-World War II literature and practices of creativity, as well as the various ways it has been assessed and taught in the past, reveals a mixed bag of operating assumptions:

1. Everyone has the potential for creativity.
2. Innovation can be taught.
3. No one approach works.
4. Multiplicity rules.
5. Generally, innovation eludes assessment.

Did it work? It stirred the pot, shook things up, was often fun, but generally did not produce results commensurate with the investment or its grandiose claims sufficient to ensure continuance. Above all, the rigors of return on investment were never included in the evaluation equation. Although there are many reasons for both its popularity and demise, the principal one is that it was not needy enough.

Competition was not as intense as it is now, and productivity was not a compelling goal. There was little insistence on a more explicit and urgent linkage of innovation to business objectives. The other problem was obsessive guru focus. All eggs were put in one basket—in the brilliant concepts and exercises of a de Bono, for example—which violated one of its own commandments. Finally, not unlike its distance from practical applications, innovation as a cognitive faculty was generally isolated and enjoyed star status. Thus, it was not linked to its kinship faculties that could ensure wider application and access to diverse learning styles and modes.

Nevertheless, the five assumptions constitute a workable starting point to guide current and future innovation training. But they need to be extended with the following supplements:

6. Existing instruments for assessing innovation capacity are valid and still can be used. (Myers Briggs, after all, classifies kinds of thinking.)
7. Developing new tests for innovation may have to wait and be informed by the findings of brain research, cognitive psychology, and genetic studies.
8. Across-the-board innovation training must yield wider company results if it is to be justified.
9. Innovation thus has to be linked to the ways we think, our modes of inquiry, and finally the rich diversity of learning pathways.
10. Innovation training is threshold training.

To honor all of the above requires a special strategy of deflection. Innovation should not be attacked head-on but surrounded by multiple and reinforcing approaches—three in particular: ideas, questions, and multiple intelligences. Innovation is too elusive on the one hand and too clever on the other to be obviously tricked into making itself easily available or usable. Innovation is an artful dodger that eludes the grasp of singular or linear-sequential approaches. But it can be accessed by ideas, questions, and multiple intelligences.

Even Thomas Edison found creativity intimidating. So, rather than storm the barricades, he settled for thresholds to innovation. He turned instead to ideas. But lest matters remain too unspecified or be allowed to drift without closure, he divided ideas into two types: major and minor. And he required that he and all his fellow inventors operate on a quota and timetable system. Edison's was modest: one major and six minor ideas within six months.

One would have expected Edison to be more ambitious until one discerns how exacting his definition of ideas. They were to be genuinely new, unborrowed, and haunting. They could not be rehashed or absorbed from any one else. And they could not offer any easy resolution or peace. Edison kept an idea diary, as did many of his coworkers. The pages following the recording of the original idea were filled with many revisions, twists, and turns, as if the idea were writhing in agony to finally express and release itself in unexpected clarity. At that point, the idea crossed the threshold into the laboratory. That is where innovation was born.

But, of course, this was not always the case. Some ideas remained stuck in an undeveloped or unapplied state. Others clustered, complicated, and confused each other, producing a rich impasse. Like orphans or old lovers, they were even abandoned and remain unfinished still lifes. To be sure, some submerged into the unconscious, there to be suspended permanently or until another idea summoned their reengagement and resurfacing. But so many shared a fate of suspension that one can better understand why Edison settled for only one major idea and six major ones. Only the strongest and most tenacious could survive the idea gauntlet. And even some of those subsequently failed to see the light of day.

Using Edison as our model and ideas as the means to innovation, what then are the essential ingredients of an intellectual IQ—an ideas quotient? Minimally, three: curiosity, persistence, and surprise. The dilemma is that idea curiosity is rare in adults, especially big ideas. Like enthusiasm and delight, it has been usually disciplined out of us during our early years in school. The MBA continues the process by enshrining the conventional current holies. To rediscover the power and spontaneity of idea curiosity requires an understanding of the thinking and learning processes of childhood.

A child expresses his curiosity through play. Learning is child's play. But although that was acceptable before school (sometimes, sadly, not even then), formal schooling marks the time to put away our play and get down to real work. School, like a job, is serious business and cannot be taken lightly. It perhaps recalls the difficult question Huck Finn put to Tom Sawyer: "Why is it that kids are good but many adults are bad?" Tom answers philosophically, "They just grow up." Shortly after that, Huck decides not to be civilized by Aunt Sally but instead lights out for the territory ahead—the West—so that he can remain permanently a child.

The key to recovering curiosity is to reintroduce serious and exacting play into work—to bring to the job what we do outside of the job. The current preoccupation with balancing work and life might be enriched and better directed by such an exchange. I paraphrase Frost, who rightly claimed, "My ambition is to make my avocation my vocation and my vocation my avocation." To make play work means process-driven training: scenarios, simulations, role-playing, scripting, teaming—all hands-on. But it all has to be involving, exhibit verisimilitude, and be work specific. Generic trust exercises won't cut it. The goal is to refresh the eyes, the ears, and even the heart to perceive the daily, ordinary, and habitual exchanges of work with a child's way of problem stating and solving.

Play has to be shown as raising the ante, as muscular engagement, not as trivial pursuit or indulgence. It uses a child's mind to roam and do mischief in the adult world of knowledge, ideas, and work assumptions. But because it is always directed toward problem solving, play needs to generate adult ideas and engage adult persistence lest the child's capacity for distraction and novelty rule. An idea thus becomes child's play grown up. It is big but focused, generalized but detailed, and fuses forest and trees.

Adult persistence appears in application. That extends and disciplines play into work. Curiosity is preserved but now is applied to problem solving.

Adult takeover is signaled by the appearance of ideas, but all movement forward is cumulative. Play is not left behind but subsumed. The child and adult coexist. The recovery is so seamless that it is not possible to determine where the one begins and the other leaves off. Innovation, in short, is born of the fusion of ideas and play or rather idea play.

Another characteristic of the curiosity of the child is asking questions, endlessly. Although again and often, sadly, that capacity too often is compromised. Schooling, impatient and busy parents at home, and supervisors at work sadly squelch and suppress questions. Indeed, when frowns or other forms of disapproval appear, the questions stop being asked altogether. Then, too, mixed signals often reinforce silence: a question is asked by one of the bright rising stars and is immediately welcomed when that is exactly the same one put forth earlier by one less favored. Gradually, fear and unfairness produce silence. The famous "road not taken" becomes the "question not asked."

Questioning is another form of play. In the child it carries no limits or responsibility. Questions just pour out, pell-mell, in a hit-and-miss fashion. They beget others ad infinitum that roam all over the place. But that is what play is: it has no purpose other than being playful. But questions are curiosity embodied now in language. As such it is the way the child thinks and the way he (or she) finds and expresses his first ideas and forms his first relationships.

Questions and ideas need not only to be paired but also to become avenues to and versions of each other. The idea quotient (IQ) has to be supplemented with a question quotient (QQ). The focus on innovation has to involve stirring systematic questioning technique and applications. The larger institutional goal is to create a questioning culture.

Questioning has a number of creative functions and applications. First, they are answers to questions. When Ben Gurion was asked shortly after Israel became a nation what it was like to be prime minister, he answered with the question: "What is it like to be prime minister of a country in which everyone thinks he is the prime minister?"

Other than being politically astute, the point of using a question to respond to a question is to shift the focus from the leader to those ostensibly being led and thus provide more information than we would have had if the question had been simply and directly answered. In other words, answering questions with questions builds and expands the knowledge base. It is a data-gathering process. It also can be an innovating process when the question is given over to the problem.

An MIT exercise to facilitate team training also inadvertently was creative. A group of automobile engineers with various expertise was assembled to identify the energy demands of their respective components. When totaled up, the battery was dead. The group was then asked to function as a team but this time to become the battery. Each component was served, and the battery remained viable.

The battery had different needs and constraints from those who used it. When the subjects became that object, not only did their questions change but they also solved the problem. Teaming only involved the number involved. It did not generate the solution. One person becoming the battery could bring about the same happy result. The key was shifting the ground so that questions ruled.

Questions also facilitate changing identities. They can structure crossover. They enable the problem solver to ask how the problem would solve itself, and then go quiet and listen to the answer. Innovation often requires being a conduit, a messenger taking orders from a battery or a computer program or a customer. The invention is always bigger than the inventor.

But even when questions do not yield solutions, they often gather the information that is the key to problem solving. Perhaps the classic expression of that yield was the typical way Louis B. Mayer began his conversations: "For your information, let me ask you a question." Questions are tyrannical. They demand answers. And if the questions are tough and have been worked up to the state of the art, they can generate information that significantly expands the knowledge base.

For example, one exercise in innovation training that would convey both the informational and creative power of questioning would require all attending to assemble a list of frequently asked questions (FAQ) for a new product or process. Or to anticipate and prepare a Q&A list for a stockholders meeting, a merger, or the press. Varying the audience ups the extent, range, and depth of the questions, but all expose ignorance, limited understanding, and questionable assumptions. And all of these singly or collectively preclude innovation.

If the holy grail is granted only to the pure of heart, innovation comes only to the endless questioners. Ignorance and ego mutually block or blunt the process. Questions take care of both by taking us outside of the box of ourselves and limiting assumptions. The process is one of increasingly using information and insight to bring about a coincidence of inventor and invention, of problem and solution.

Questions also can be systematically structured. The Japanese approach to problem solving involves getting at the root cause. When something breaks down or when targets are not met, the Japanese ask why at least five times to reach bedrock. The limits of each partial answer and stage compel further inquiry until finality occurs. Because such questioning is regarded as a neutral agent of inquiry by all, the blame, shame, and gotcha game are not involved. Indeed, if such questioning becomes a norm, it also becomes company culture. It is its mission.

But even when absent, it can be created. How the creative power of questioning can be developed and the culture changed is sometimes surprisingly easy. One such example is provided by Kendall Murphy when he was asked to take over a major division of Pacific Bell that regularly had failed to meet target goals.

Murphy's reputation as a rapid turnaround manager led to the appointment. Typically, he was a hard-nosed, blunt, and top-down leader who took charge. This time, however, he slowed down and took a more indirect approach. The division was the biggest, staffed by the cream of the crop, and required a technical expertise that Murphy did not possess. So rather that using his proven technique of immediately shaking things up and shifting supervisors around, he kept all his direct reports in place. He attended all their meetings, raised issues, and made notes of what he would include in his change plan.

But at the end of the month, he was startled when the numbers appeared. Every unit had made gains. Some even met target goals; one exceeded. He was bewildered and called all his direct reports together. They came to the meeting bouncy but wary. Murphy wanted to know what had happened. No one answered. He pressed harder. Still no response. Finally, he turned on the supervisor of the worst performing unit in the past and demanded an answer.

Rather sheepishly the supervisor said, "We did nothing. But I think it had something to do with your attendance at our meetings. You began by asking us questions that had never been asked before. And you kept up the barrage at all the subsequent meetings. After you left, we spent hours trying to come up with answers that we planned to offer you at our next meeting. But by then you went off on a tear of different questions that we had to add to our agenda. So if you are looking for an answer for the turnaround, it has to do with your use of the third degree that we in turn applied to ourselves." Murphy was stunned into humbled silence and changed totally the way he planned to introduce change in the future.

The classic formula of problem solving is Know-What, Know-How, and Know-Why. Kendall Murphy's law is that the last needs to be first.

Questions and ideas need to drive everything else. And further when that is done collectively and systematically, it leads to information sharing that ultimately evolves into leadership sharing. If an organization is stuck and asks, "When was the last time we came up with a new idea?," then it is time to develop a questioning culture, if for no other reason than not to be paralyzed by such an unanswered question.

Questions can start new businesses and tap new markets, as well as maintain, renew, and energize existing ones. And if they don't, companies may wake up one morning to find their breakfast eaten by another whose new ideas generated quality questions as their competitive edge.

One last member of the innovative trinity of ideas and questions needs to be brought into play. And that involves multiple intelligences (MI), especially as identified and defined by its original inventor, Howard Gardner. Aside from explicitly linking MI to creativity, Gardner enriches the entire process of innovation by bringing minimally two dimensions to bear on training.

The first requires the recognition that every employee is multiply talented. The second shifts the question from "How smart am I?" to "How am I smart?" That change of focus from standard and singular intelligence quotient to a process-oriented and multiple world of ideas and questions signals a change from analysis to creativity, from incremental productivity to discontinuous innovation.

What Gardner argued is that we are not only adaptive but multiply so. We grow and know not only in one way but also in many and diverse ways and along multiple learning pathways. Finally, the internal cognitive world that stirs creativity is as busy and interactive as what it creates. Gardner conceded that Western civilization in general had achieved distinction for the most part through linguistically driven analysis. He argued that that was not only more involved but that what was often passed off as solely the process of verbal dominance was in reality multiply produced. Indeed, the driving spark was often nonverbal.

In his seminal work *Frames of Mind* (1983) (a significant title), Gardner identified seven (later eight) basic intelligences: linguistic, musical, logical-mathematical, spatial, bodily-kinesthetic, interpersonal, intrapersonal, and naturalist. In later discussions of optimal human adaptability, Gardner stresses the existential and the futuristic, rounding it out to ten intelligences.

What does MI bring to innovation?

- All humans are multiply configured.
- The design is wired in the brain and biology.
- Current IQ is singular and thus reductive. It measures only linguistic intelligence.
- All intelligences are multiply operative in preschool children.
- They appear as playful development of simple and basic ideas and questions.
- Such a gradual expanding knowledge base is common to all children and constitutes the lifelong legacy of the species.
- The three principal and preferred activities of MI are communication (socialization), problem solving, and creativity.
- But they all are routinely goal directed and directional.
- When schools build onto the acquired common-knowledge base, continue to tap the multiple talents that produced it, and set end goals of inquiry and achievement focused on optimal adaptability, that brings fully into play the three fundamental activities of communication, problem solving, and creativity.

Gardner's educational mission was to argue for a continuum, not a break, between preschool and school, and to employ MI as the bridging agent. In the process, a number of MI schools were established and have been successful. But Gardner's proposals have not been applied to business, and his notion of MI has generally remained untapped by and for training. It is an unfortunate sin of omission because it already incorporates the contributions of ideas and questions on the one hand, and defines the center of human activity as problem solving and creativity on the other hand.

How then can MI be used to stir and advance innovation? One of its principal contributions is serving as a constant multiplier. The intelligences constitute a circular checklist of problem definition. Each intelligence would generate its own version. The problem would thus be surrounded and immediately enriched by a cast of characters and a range of statements that ideally would be 360 degrees. Later on, such a comprehensive matrix can be flipped over and applied to the solution.

Routinely, such a dynamic also establishes or renews each employee's relationships with different and many ways of knowing, thinking, and learning. Access to a richer interior world is initially bracing, subsequently familiar, and regularly extending. Each employee is bigger and thus more equal and fortified to stretch work tasks and goals.

The inherent interoperability of MI also facilitates crossovers of perspective and function. It can do so because it not only can externally display the multiple complexities of the company in miniature but can also make them interoperable. MI would have considerably eased the exchange of positions of the automotive engineers and the battery. And because Gardner has factored in the interpersonal and intrapersonal, the groundwork for incorporating emotional intelligence also has been laid and even anticipated.

Above all, MI ups the ante. It requires the three basic activities to be constantly reciprocal, almost interchangeable. Communications has to be problem solving and creative. Problem solving has to be communicative and innovative. Creativity must exhibit communicability and solve problems. Ordinarily, each task would be a separate operation, but in MI's enriched environment they are all contiguous and interfacing. The MI world is always finally holistic, and its innovative creations, when and if they come, emerge fully formed and complete. Singular approaches limited to singular intelligence routinely pass off halves as wholes. If innovation is the company mission, MI constitutes its vision.

In summary, then, two changes are being advocated. First, if innovation can be taught, it can be done so only obliquely and through kinship allies. The thresholds proposed are those of ideas, questions, and multiple intelligences. All three lend themselves to systemic application and thus not only offer uniform and comprehensive use across the board but also are amenable and receptive to individual and company original signatures. Second, for innovation to take hold and be a driving force, it must bring together or unite the three essentials of communication, problem solving, and creativity. Reciprocity between all three will produce a holistic vision that ultimately may be the most enduring, embracing, and reverberating innovation of all to all.

Perhaps the most difficult obstacle to overcome is not so much the content innovation training but the context. The fusion of testing and training requires the trainer constantly to assess the extent and to track the ways that ideas, questions, and MI emerge and contribute to creative growth. In other words, the conventional external and follow-up evaluation of the implementation and application of training to work

now appears earlier and is part of the internal process of the training itself. Aside from adding a new and difficult dimension to the complexity
of instructional design, how could e-learning accommodate supplemental evaluation, especially self-contained CD training?

But that is what always happens. When the universe is disturbed,
everything changes. We created programs that were essentially autonomous and self-teaching. They were the best composites of best
practices and thus state of the art. The "instructor" was the program, a
superior virtual amalgam and substitute for face-to-face reality. Un-
evenness was evened out, wayward digressions kept on task, and return
on investment was documented. Now there is a new challenge: asking e-
learning to fuse testing and training.

To a large extent, that is not new. Many e-learning programs test for
comprehension along the way. But that assesses overt and outward
knowledge and understanding, not the process of how it came about.
How to get behind the surface to substance, the static results to the dynamics of how they were produced, is the new task of innovation training focused on ideas, questions, and MI.

One approach is an obvious but daunting solution. Since what is to
be known and assessed belongs to and is intimate with those being
trained, what ways can be explored and found for self-examination and
self-measurement? Is it possible to turn the task over to employee self-
reflection, to making those trained the trainer?

REFERENCES

Frost, Robert. 1969. *The Poetry of Robert Frost: The Complete Poems, Complete and Unabridged.* Edited by Edward C. Latham. New York: Henry Holt.
Gardner, Howard. 1983. *Frames of mind: The theory of multiple intelligences.*
New York: Basic Books.
———. 1991. *The unschooled mind: How children think and how schools should
teach.* New York: Basic Books.
———. 1993. *Multiple intelligences: The theory in practice.* New York: Basic
Books.
Twain, Mark. 1989. *The Adventures of Huckleberry Finn.* New York: Tom Doherty. (Originally published 1884.)

30

BREAKING UP
INNOVATION LOG JAMS

Things refuse to be mismanaged long.

—Ralph Waldo Emerson

Consultants regularly have to listen to the lamentations of clients: detailed descriptions of political intrigue, upper-level upstaging and back-stabbing, impossible goals to reach, and, above all, martyrdom: "I am so busy I don't have time to go to the restroom." "My plate is so full I am behind on all of my assignments." "My boss just gave me another task; I guess it will be late nights every week for the next month at least." "I bring work home every weekend. I take it to soccer games, even museums." And so on.

Alas, it's all true. The dream of the reduced work week and of a leisurely future has just not happened. Professionals are working harder and longer than ever before. Although as consultants we listen sympathetically and allow our clients to vent, we seldom press the matter home and suggest that perhaps the problem of overload should be given a higher priority by HR, examined, and, if possible, fixed. However, in a perhaps unexpected and yet typical way, that issue refused to stay buried and resurfaced in a surprising way.

When we pressed one of our besieged clients who was in charge of innovation, what emerged was an obstruction that in turn hid a mother lode. The senior manager was responsible largely for bringing on new products and services and had an excellent reputation in the industry for being effective in that role. He also regularly complained about being overworked, but clearly it was not incapacitating. So what was the secret of his success? After singing the praises of the CEO and saluting the flag again and again, he confessed, "We hire good people, get out of their way, and gain share." We were all in a state of admiration: "No wonder you work hard. That is no easy task. But look at what you produced!" Then he dropped the other shoe. He whipped out a fat folder, jammed with papers, and waved it in our faces: "Yeah, but what about all these proposals for innovation? Some of them are over a year old. And I can't get to them." We asked to borrow the folder and made an appointment to see him the next day.

What emerged was fascinating. Even lacking sufficient technical expertise to evaluate accurately the some 100 proposals, we had no difficulty picking at least 25 winners. We lamented that so many companies seem to have such difficulties in generating new and creative approaches, and here this firm (and perhaps many others) is up to its ears in innovative people. But it does have a problem with blockage. It can't get things flowing. It can't seem to get the ideas out of the folder and into the lab or onto the factory floor or whatever to test them and see whether they are feasible or not.

But what could we suggest? Clearly, we could not return the next day and tell the overworked senior manager to work harder. So we decided we had to become more innovative ourselves and generate a solution that would not add to his burdens but lighten the load of expediting innovation. The analysis below is what we came up with

I. STRUCTURING IMPLEMENTATION

Creativity is minimally a three-step process. The first is coming up with the idea. The second is testing its feasibility. The third is making it happen. So many firms are so beset by finding ways to stir innovation that they forget the other two parts. And then suddenly they find ideas stillborn, and their employees resentful about what has happened or not happened to their "babies." (Even engineers have egos.)

The irony, however, is that most organizations that need and value innovation are not structurally innovative themselves. They have the same old pyramids of vertical transit and transmittal. Everything usually funnels to the same senior vice president. He may have one or two lower-level assistants with limited expertise and with even more limited authority and who clearly are outclassed. In fact, the moment an employee learns that it has been given to one of the assistants, he concludes, not incorrectly, that the bureaucracy is alive and well and that nothing will happen. And for the most part, he is correct.

There is thus a structural mismatch. Innovation is free flowing, whereas chain of command is static escalation. They metaphorically are on a collision course. Flow has to meet flow. To be sure, it may have to be adjusted, but it still has to be in motion and ongoing. So the first major change is structural. The senior vice president's office has to be reconceived as a way station, not a permanent stopping place. It functions not unlike a railway turntable. It is where things are logged in, profiled, and logged out. To where? To whom?

2. INTERNAL OUTSOURCING

The senior vice president in charge of innovation is responsible for developing a follow-up evaluative format. It is the work of diverse hands: planning, production, human resources, budget, marketing, sales, and so forth. It also needs to be run through the vision and mission statements to make sure it is compatible. Indeed, both of these have to be added to the evaluation as a check-off category. After it has been massaged and critiqued, it is cast in three forms. One simple—ideally one page—fast and dirty checklist to see if it passes basic review. The second is more advanced and thorough but still limited in terms of depth. The third is complex and exhaustive and develops in detail the categories of the second review and focuses them on action.

The company uses internal reviewers, preferably innovative types, who have submitted their own ideas. They are limited to the first evaluative cut. Turnaround time is no longer than two weeks. They tally the scores, present their conclusions, and make recommendations. They are given a code to use instead of their name. A copy of each evaluation is fed back to the innovative employee.

The second stage is also internal. An innovation review team consisting of one representative from each of the major areas/categories has two weeks to determine whether it is a go or not, and, if the former, whether it is to be designated for the fast track.

Ideally, the entire initial review process should take no more than four weeks. In the process, employees will become more sensitive to what management is looking for when it reviews innovation. The different divisions will all share in the process and hopefully promote more interdivisional understanding and cooperation. And the senior vice president will just have to review recommendations, not unreviewed proposals.

3. EXTERNAL OUTSOURCING

If the company has a happy problem—too many new or complex ideas to process at a good pace—then a stable of external reviewers and consultants should be maintained and used. These would be invaluable when an innovation is involved in an area that exceeds the internal expertise of the company. They also can be called upon for a second opinion when a proposal has been given a mixed or borderline rating. And periodically they should be called in as a team to review past reviews.

Our proposals were accepted. We then were asked to develop a budget estimating the costs of implementing innovation. We did not wish to doom the project before it could get off the ground by asking for new money. We recommended that a percentage of gain sharing be taken off the top to fund the process. The proposal was accepted, and within a month things began to hum.

Listening to martyrdom is sometimes therapeutic—but only when one gets beyond the sources of the stigmata and strikes pay dirt. That is when consultants are really helpful, earn their keep, and bring considerable added value to their clients. But innovation ideas have to meet innovation structures for the marriage to be blessed with offspring. In other words, whether or not MI is tapped as a springboard for innovation, its basic resistance to singular systems and structures often brings about creative alternatives and solutions. MI multiplies options and in so doing encourages innovation.

31

BALANCING INNOVATION
AND STANDARDS

The call for innovation has become so intense, insistent, and invasive on the one hand, and so glibly assumed or proclaimed on the other hand, that unless anticipated, worried about, and planned for it has the potential to trigger a series of organizational dislocations. Here are some of the most obvious and problematic:

- *HR*: What are the key job descriptors for hiring creative types? Do they even exist?
- *Supervisors*: How is innovation to be evaluated?
- *R&D*: What happens to their traditional monopoly?
- *Senior Staff*: Should a commitment to innovation compel revisiting and perhaps revising the mission?
- *CEO*: If that top position now were invested with modeling innovation, how many current CEOs would survive the test?
- *CLO*: What happens to the standard array of offerings? What balance needs to be struck? And what is the state of art and the standards of innovation training?

Although the focus here is predictably limited to the last item, it is increasingly the characteristic fate of chief learning officers to inherit the whole ball of wax. To be sure, such 360-degree coverage may be a reassuring sign not only of the increasing centrality of training but also of the extent human capital is now the equal of financial capital in any tally of intellectual capital. But being holistic still requires seeing both the forest and the trees.

With innovation up front and in the driver's seat, a number of top-to-bottom and side-to-side transitions need to be addressed. Moreover, such an across-the-board commitment inevitably involves CLOs in a series of balancing acts that seek to serve many masters evenhandedly. What are some of the most critical balances to be struck by CLOs? The list is substantial and includes some familiar and some new items, but all are challenging.

The first is always costs. Given tight budgets, what resources are available for new program development? And should innovation be developed in-house—do we have the expertise? If outsourced, to whom?

Next is the learning-management-systems balancing act. What percentage of total offerings should be devoted to innovation? Or rather, should it be calculated differently? Instead of conceiving of innovation as an overhaul, why not an overlay, a value add-on to basic training? After all, should not a significant portion remain ongoing, incremental, and continuous? Not everything should change focus. Otherwise, a very fat tail of innovation may be wagging an anemic dog.

One of the toughest issues is evaluation. How should innovation be measured? Current standards and procedures for performance evaluation are probably inadequate. But must an entirely new system be developed from scratch? Or can a hybrid be created? In either case, both the evaluation system and the innovation being measured have to be joined at the hip when introduced in training.

Administrative issues of implementation quickly surface. Should it be selective or companywide? Creativity experts argue for the latter, pointing out that innovation is curiously democratic and capricious, often selecting the most unlikely candidates. The other tack argues against squandering resources and in the process also possibly generating disappointing expectations. What probably will win the argument for across-the-board implementation is the difficulties and complexities of defining the selection criteria. Adjusted by education, job, and level? Individual or team? Who constitutes the first wave? The greater obstacles may dictate the course of action. But whatever the final decision, the related issue of assessing employee capacity for innovation quickly surfaces as a deciding factor.

That segues to employee testing. That has significantly been urged forward by CLOs who value diagnostically driven training. But have thinking and learning profiles been factored in? Thinking certainly has in Myers-Briggs, but not learning. Besides, what needs to be determined is what patterns of learning preferences and styles are proximate to or even identical with innovation. In short, we need a test for determining innovation quotient (IQ). Or does it already exist under different names and protocols?

Balancing also requires that a relationship between productivity and innovation be renegotiated. While the holy grail of innovation is being pursued, with no guarantee of outcomes according to a fixed timetable, productivity must be maintained. Indeed, is the relationship between the two a break or a continuum? If the latter, then perhaps innovation should be considered the ultimate version of productivity—a new norm for all.

A constantly bedeviling issue is another relationship: between incentives and innovation. Traditionally, reward systems have been incremental. More earned more. And in many companies innovation similarly has been highly and visibly recognized. Even joint patents have been filed. But is innovation like sales? Do incentives really motivate, or are we dealing with a different kind of animal altogether? Maybe an extraterrestrial?

Innovation is of two types: continuous and discontinuous. The first is incremental. It is endless improvement of existing products and services. It preserves and ensures profitability. It sustains cash flow. But discontinuous innovation is out of the box. It is disruptive technology. It even has the potential to put the current organization out of business or to create a new competitive business entirely. Indeed, such a disconnect from what currently exists is not only the infallible mark of genuine innovation but also a demonstration of its fidelity to market dynamics and behaviors.

Clearly, both kinds of innovation should be pursued. Incremental reward systems should be maintained for continuous improvement. Granting a percentage share of the new business might be the appropriate way of stimulating a different and discontinuous kind of innovation. But balancing still requires a mixture of sure and steady progress and the final eureka moment. Above all, if innovation becomes a companywide commitment, then the standard process of inquiry is upped to discovery. Even if no breakthroughs occur at all or soon, such general gains benefit all and help to shape an innovative culture. Innovation is not only about the future, it is the future.

Finally, if the history of creativity training since the end of World War II is reviewed, what surfaces are the ups and downs of a faddish phenomenon. But now matters are much different. Now there is a new state of the art. Innovation is currently the object of brain research, cognitive science/psychology, and genetics. Now a variation called fMRI enables direct study of brain activity and its learning pathways while responses are given to certain triggering questions. This is not unlike current real-time data making transparent and accessible operational and decision-making processes.

Clearly, from such studies what may emerge is not only a series of ways of generally improving the effectiveness of training but also knowing what stirs the brain and its emotional makeup to combine opposites and to be innovative. The geometric growth rates between technology and cognition may thus not be not only alike but also reinforcing. Their common quantum leaps may, like innovation itself, be so reverberating and ongoing that they have to be regarded constantly as works in progress. Even their tandem relationship may result in parallel lines meeting.

What a crushing range of challenges to drop on CLOs and their LMSs! Is there any relief available? Have any or enough companies already gone through the process to provide a model or at least a series of guidelines? A number of issues of *CLO Magazine* have featured CLO profiles and case studies that have contained some examples of commitment to and success with innovation induction.

What follows below is a distillation of the essentials of those examples arranged in the form of series of first steps. The order is not prescriptive. The list is offered here as a way of moving forward in a balanced and comprehensive way. It is also generic to accommodate the variety of enterprises, the diversity of their cultures and strategic plans, and where they are at—beginning, middle, or mature stages—in the process. Minimally, there are three steps.

I. RESEARCH AND BEST PRACTICES INVENTORY

CLOs have to compile an inventory minimally in three areas. They must survey and monitor the findings of brain research, cognitive science, and genetic impacts on thinking, learning, and leading. Particular attention should be paid to the cognition publications of the MIT Press. A search for best practices requires reviewing the literature and LMS programs for current models of innovation training, especially e-versions. Often this can best be done by attending national conferences, which inevitably feature state-of-the art presentations sooner than print. In addition to the standard and familiar ones, consider attending SALT (Society for Alternative Technology).

Finally, there is the need to increase the knowledge of and commitment to employee testing and profiling. High on that list would be the development of a new IQ (innovation quotient) test. A less sensational approach would be an Idea Quotient.

As already noted, Thomas Edison gave himself and all his employees idea quotas and required them to keep idea diaries. He divided ideas into major and minor categories. The former disturbed the universe; the latter changed or refreshed the way things were done. Both operated within a six-month time table. Edison gave himself one big and six smaller ideas as his goals.

Aside from reflecting the differences between continuous and discontinuous innovation already noted, Edison wisely opted for a threshold approach. Ideas are proximate to innovation. They are inevitably embryonic. Ideas are also less intimidating and precious than creativity, but they are also rare enough to offer the road less traveled. They answer the familiar criticism: "When was the last time that organization came up with a new idea?" Idea generating thus may be the training focus for innovation training.

2. BALANCING STRATEGIES AND PRIORITIES

Balancing requires aligning and fusing continuity and discontinuity so that both kinds of innovation can be pursued separately and in parallel. The gains must always be double and doubling. In addition, productivity and innovation needs to be perceived as a continuum. Innovation is the ultimate version of productivity. Such spectrum also accommodates using innovation as an overlay rather than an overhaul of current program array.

3. IMPLEMENTATION AND EVALUATION

Consider sharing the discussion and decision of whether to implement selectively or across the board with senior staff and divisional heads. Minimally, seek consensus on who would go first and why. Follow that with divisional receptivity and particularly with their recommendations of specialized contributions to innovation.

Whether implementation is partial or total, evaluation has to be across the board. Whether a supplement or completely new system is developed, innovation has to become a performance norm for every one. Its application would range from new hires to retirement (normal or hastened). It would be minimally a double-layered structure. It would contain both companywide criteria as well as specific divisional or specialization standards, as long as those latter expectations neither exceeded nor fell below those of the company as whole. Innovation would be defined as the ultimate stage of productivity and be included in all job descriptions.

This all may appear to be quite a bit to ask of current chief learning officers and their learning management systems, but it now goes with the expanded territory. Besides, given the prospect of dramatically changing the cultural focus of an entire enterprise and presiding over its critical transition, CLOs need to recall and be braced by the call of Toynbee: "The greater the challenge, the greater the response." In many ways, the challenge of innovation, especially balancing its many linkages and alignments, may signal that the time is ripe for CLOs and their LMSs to come into their own.

But one note of caution. Innovation has to be treated with kid gloves—almost with reverence. It is more mystery than mastery. It is different not just in degree but in kind from standard and incremental knowledge acquisition. Without appearing precious, at one extreme innovation is incandescent—the realm of mystics and artists. At the other extreme, it is the ultimate triumph of problem solving. But neither is produced by those who are comfortable with routine operations and habitual language.

32

IMITATION, INTUITION, AND INNOVATION

Recently, Eric Bonabeau (2004) described and documented the extent to which we have become increasingly an imitative society. Mimicking the pursuit of success and acceptance, he claims, has led to self-gratifying behaviors that are often mindless. To be sure, this is nothing new. Throughout, time, we have frequently been swept up in historical hysterias, whether they involved medieval or McCarthy witch hunts or the feeding frenzy of stock market buying and selling. Herd thinking leads to herd actions in all arenas, political, commercial, financial, or technical.

Unfortunately, imitation is also negatively affecting other areas of achievement. It thus has led to questioning the value of seeking consensus. Is it a genuine triumph of negotiation or a really fast and dirty herd agreement in disguise? Even best practices may be suspect. When emulated and imitated, are they in the long run a way of inhibiting development beyond the current state of the art of the status quo? Under the pressure of imitation, do best practices undermine and preclude innovation?

According to Bonabeau, there are four factors that drive imitation. The first is safety—being with all the others doing the same thing. There is thus safety in numbers, disaster in being alone. Bonabeau (2004) quotes McKinsey's Charles Roxburgh: "For most CEOs, only one thing is worse than making a huge strategic mistake: being the only one in the industry to make it."

The second is conformity—doing at least what every one of your competitors is doing so that you can always say to customers, "We can provide that." To be sure, it may not make sense for you to offer it. The internal resources may not even be available, but still imitation minimally requires matching the range of the competition so that one does not appear deficient.

The third force of "me-too-ism" is success by association. We believe that those who are successful should be followed. They evidently know where the pot of gold is, better than we do. Such knee-jerk thinking or nonthinking has led many American companies to join the bonanza of going global. In the process, they posted overseas losses that had to be absorbed by their domestic operations.

Finally, there is good old-fashioned greed. The prospect of missing or being left out compels companies and their CEOs to do what the winners and the stars do. Routinely shortsighted, it often places solid companies in vulnerable positions and commits them to a direction not in keeping with their core mission. Occasionally, greed even can consume the market itself, with each one adding just one more sheep—resulting in the "tragedy of the commons."

Lest consolation can be taken in being forewarned, Bonabeau goes on to describe in great detail how marketing experts already are tapping into and exploiting the forces of imitation. Increasingly, the process of being programmed to mimic the safe and successful is being refined and accelerated to the point where we are becoming a society that does not re-create but imitates itself.

It may not be limited to externals or market manipulation. It may also characterize internal company cultures as well. How many organizations evidence a kind of thinking that is preeminently safe, conformist, success worshipping, and envious? How often are organizational views and plans stirred and structured by an orientation that is excessively outward facing and preoccupied by imitating or following the passing parade of fads and fashions of their competitors? How worshipful have we become of compilations of the best companies, and how are we are driven to emulate these stars? And, finally, what chance, if any, does genuine innovation have of taking hold and overcoming both the counterfeits offered by imitation and the best practices of the trendsetters?

Taking on and redirecting the excessive imitative behaviors and thinking of company cultures is formidable for many reasons. First, we have not generally done this. The perils of imitation is not a familiar or typical subject of discourse or training. Second, the tiger is both inside and outside the gates. Internal mimicking is mirrored by external reinforcement. Resistance may be total. Third, imitation is not always inherently flawed. It has accounted for considerable success. So unless ambiguity rules and imitation is cast as both hero and villain, credibility may be undermined. Finally, it is not enough to target and expose imitation. There must be a bigger or larger replacement goal. The one that makes the most sense, given the pernicious influence of imitation on the one hand and the overriding needs of companies on the other hand, is innovation.

The key strategy is for training to take on the task of addressing imitation. Separate workshops may be designed, overlays to existing ones may be added, or both developed. Equally as important is implementation. Such training should become a staple of new-employee orientation. Indeed, they could even be used as preemployment screening to inform applicants of company expectations. To ensure companywide diffusion, however, the new recommended performance behaviors and thinking need to be made part of all evaluation systems.

But for the training to be effective, it must be progressively inclusive. First, it requires that we address thinking directly. The dynamics of the thinking process becomes the examined mental metrics. Second, behavior not only has to be added, but thinking and behavior also have to be fused. It is a two-way street. How we act is also how we think, and how we think is also how we behave. How we make decisions and problem solve reflects both process and end points. Ultimately, thinking is behavior. Third, learning is added to the mix. Mimicking is presented as a key and legitimate form of learning from childhood on, but it can be deceptive just as our senses are often suspect. A corrective process begins, which involves examining and questioning the thinking assumptions and behaviors involved in the four major drivers of imitation. But what is critical throughout is encouraging examination and examples, drawn as Bonabeau does from personal experience. Unless that is done, the pervasive extent of imitation will not be acknowledged. Such a process then concludes with the emergence of independent thinking as the antidote to slavish imitative thinking.

This marks a crucial juncture. Typically, independent thinking would be a sufficiently legitimate end point. It is inherently corrective of the excesses of imitation. It provides a more balanced perspective, relies on data and documentation, and generally ensures more solid and robust decision making and problem solving. Independent thinking is what produces and sustains best practices. As such, it is a familiar and final respectable position for those companies that do not wish to venture into chancier and often uncharted waters.

Independence, though admirable, is also limited. It is too self-possessed, too much in charge and in control of itself and others to take the next step of surrender. Independence is not innovation. And just as excessive imitation often requires independent thinking as a corrective, so excessive independence may require intuition as the bridge to innovation. Thus, if the decision is to go for the whole ball of wax, we are now confronted with the ironic dilemma of transforming our final goal into an intermediate one and persuading our independent thinkers to surrender part of their independence to intuition.

Just as thinking and behavior have to be fused, so do intuition and innovation. Innovation is perhaps the ultimate version of problem with this difference: the whole is greater than the sum of its parts. For that to happen, the problem must be bigger—not just a problem but the problem of problems so that the solution solves all versions of the problem. In many ways, the problem is left behind as a single and separate construct and becomes instead a distilled and unified essential. It becomes a big all-inclusive question or enigma. Intuition takes it into a realm that is still and timeless. It is pure present or the future, defined solely as all now. Indeed, when innovation occurs, so does the future. Innovation creates the future; so much so that sometimes it is discontinuous and even disruptive of the present and its solutions.

Every innovation ultimately drives markets. It always potentially creates a new business for the current one or, if rejected, is taken up by a competitor and ends that business. Thus, new ways of doing things becomes new ways of doing business and, perhaps, the creation of new businesses as a way of doing new things.

Inevitably, new ideas and innovations become businesses, so perhaps another key approach to independent thinking is entrepreneurial thinking. The wheel does not have to be reinvented. The rich literature of entrepreneurship can be tapped, and managers and employees can be asked to create not just new ideas in the abstract but new businesses that may serve not only to extend the life and diversity of the current company but also to give it a new future.

The additional piece to be added to independent thinking then is entrepreneurial thinking. That also enjoys the additional value of employees not being put off or feeling inadequate by the challenge of intuition and innovation. But following the good example of 3M, the exploratory process should be private and unmonitored. Company time should be allotted each day—3M gave 15 minutes—to indicate its value, but there is no timetable or deadline. As to which entrepreneurial model to follow, happily there are over 25 outstanding undergraduate and graduate programs from which to choose. But don't just imitate.

REFERENCE

Bonabeau, Eric. 2004. The perils of the imitation age. *Harvard Business Review* (June).

CONCLUSION:
THE 21ST-CENTURY AGENDA

The agenda of the 21st century increasingly will be holistic. Minimally, it will include the future, multiple intelligences/learning diversity, and innovation. Individually and collectively, these will define the critical options for professionals and organizations. But such foresight, cognition, and creativity need to be interoperable. Each one participates in and impinges on the other. Like Wilson's consilience, convergence rules.

Thus the future is essentially multimodal and innovative, diverse not singular. Anticipatory leadership and management thrive on the alternatives of the probable, the possible, and the aspirational. Innovation not only hastens, it coexists with the future. Breakthrough ideas and technology also create new businesses or processes that, if recognized and incorporated, give existing organizations a future lease on life; if not, they become the competition.

But to gain the benefits of multiplicity and creativity, a new relationship with the future must be formed. It cannot be the old top-down dominating relationship in which an obedient servant is given the marching orders of traditional strategic planning. Nor can one safely stand in the protective present insulated from and trying to tame the uncertainty that lies ahead. The future has to become an alter ego—better still, a secret sharer. Fortunately, access to such otherness is facilitated by multimodal and innovative thinking, learning, and leading.

Multiple intelligences and learning diversity, by virtue of combining progressive and circular thinking and problem solving, set up their students and adherents for functioning effectively in both external and internal worlds. In addition, their constant insistence on processing data and knowledge through multiple lenses makes their students and adherents comfortable with alternatives, the basic stuff of futures and innovation. Above all, as demonstrated in many MI schools, MI has become a self-conscious learning system. It is self-organizing, self-monitoring, and self-managing. In addition, it is self-amplifying.

The learning range is constantly increased as more dominant intelligences enlist and strengthen more peripheral ones to become involved and offer their difference. As a result, MI is not merely a way of explaining how we think, learn, and lead. It is also a self-directed and self-contained system of learning to learn and even unlearn, lifelong. As such, it is perhaps the optimum way of structuring a proactive and multiple relationship with the future and employing innovation as the ultimate version of problem solving.

As with futurity and MI, innovation similarly is beset by a number of basic misunderstandings and misconceptions. As some of the case examples revealed, it is regarded as easy and fast, or reserved only for the privileged creative types of R&D. Its implementation is often hurried and crude in order to guarantee results. However, no matter the difficulties and organizational obstacles, creativity cannot be ignored or made peripheral. Its ties to the future provide a lifeline of continuity to such an extent that futurity and innovation become versions of each other.

What also has emerged in the examination of creativity is the need to create the conditions and prepare the way for innovation. Although many rites of passage are available and productive, they all minimally require a basic redefinition and reorientation of both our external and internal worlds. The external has to absorb transition as a new permanent norm. Indeed, that also defines the future. The internal world is just as variegated and rich. It is the world of ideas, multiply perceived and rendered by the dynamics of many intelligences collectively involved in understanding and problem solving. As noted, the question shifts from "How smart am I?" to "How am I smart?" Building on that

MI system, we now can add that "How innovative am I?" changes to "How am I innovative?"

If we reconceive our relationship to the future, expand our notions of how we think, learn, and lead, and approach innovation as more mystery than mastery, then the promise of synthesis may be within our grasp; and the 21st century in turn may appear less as a disruptive antagonist and more as a collaborative partner.

ABOUT THE AUTHOR

Dr. Irving H. Buchen is Associate Vice President of Academic Affairs and Director of International Programs for IMPAC University, a member of the doctoral business faculty of Capella University, a Senior Principal of Canis Learning System, and training editor of *The Futurist*, the official publication of the World Future Society.

OTHER ROWMAN & LITTLEFIELD EDUCATION TITLES BY IRVING H. BUCHEN

The Future of the American School System (2004)

Parents' Guide to Student Success: Home and School Partners in the Twenty-First Century (2004)

The Future Workforce: The 21st-Century Transformation of Leaders, Managers, and Employees (2005)